JAGUA

James Mann

motorbooks

JAGUAR CARS

JAMES MANN

Jaguar
XKSS

motorbooks

ACKNOWLEDGMENTS

With thanks to the following people and organizations for allowing me to photograph their cars or giving permission to use their images in this book.

The owners:
David Hill
John Burton
Michael Byng
Mike Taylor
Trevor Burrows

Grahame Bull
Gary and Tom Robinson
Alan Giddins
Tim Allard

The Jaguar Heritage Trust
Jaguar Land Rover
Tim Bulley at *Classic and Sports Car* magazine
Ian Dawson
Swallows Independent Jaguar
Eagle E-Types

Quarto is the authority on a wide range of topics.
Quarto educates, entertains and enriches the lives of our readers—enthusiasts and lovers of hands-on living.
www.quartoknows.com

First published in 2015 by Motorbooks, an imprint of Quarto Publishing Group USA Inc., 400 First Avenue North, Suite 400, Minneapolis, MN 55401 USA.

© 2015 Quarto Publishing Group USA Inc.
All photography by James Mann

Motorbooks titles are also available at discounts in bulk quantity for industrial or sales-promotional use. For details write to Special Sales Manager at Quarto Publishing Group USA Inc., 400 First Avenue North, Suite 400, Minneapolis, MN 55401 USA.

To find out more about our books, visit us online at www.motorbooks.com.

ISBN: 978-0-7603-4842-0

Library of Congress Cataloging-in-Publication Data

Mann, James, 1963-
  Jaguar cars / James Mann.
    pages cm
  ISBN 978-0-7603-4842-0 (sc)
  1. Jaguar automobile--History. I. Title.
  TL215.J3M36 2015
  629.222--dc23

                                    2015024374

Acquiring Editor: Zack Miller
Project Manager: Sherry Anisi
Art Director: Brad Springer
Cover Designer: Karl Laun
Layout Designer: Kazuko Collins

On the front cover: F-Type
On the back cover: **Top:** SS100. **Middle:** E-Type Series III V-12. **Bottom:** C-X16
On the title page: XKSS

Printed in China

10 9 8 7 6 5 4 3 2 1

CONTENTS

INTRODUCTION &

ORIGINS

Jaguar's story of great successes and failures on the road and racetrack reflects the highs and lows of the British motor industry throughout the twentieth century. It began with one man, William Lyons, whose vision built the great marque we know and love today. Lyons recognized what the car-buying public wanted and was able to deliver it at the right price to have customers queuing around the block. His sense of style, and interest in speed, were driving forces in the company that emerged.

As a young motorcycle enthusiast living in Blackpool, England, Lyons met a fabricator building sidecars in a shed behind his parents' house. Unlike the boxy aberration typical of the time, William Walmsley's coachbuilt creations featured sleek, cigar-shaped aluminum bodies. Lyons fell in love with their racy lines and saw a bright future for them. So in 1922, the two men formed Swallow Sidecars.

Lyons was convinced that the name of a fast, graceful animal would present the right image. He was proved right about the name and the product. The company soon had to move to new premises to meet demand. Yet motorcycle sidecars was a seasonal business at the time, and Lyons believed they could do better. A more profitable future for the company would be to build motorcars, using the skilled craftsmen they had in the sidecar business.

Walmsley was a great stylist, and the young Lyons learned a lot from the older man. In 1927, with the addition of some experienced coachbuilders from the Midlands—already the center for the British car industry—the first Swallow-bodied cars were built. They used the popular and inexpensive Austin 7 chassis.

The new car proved to be highly competitive at only £175, just £10 more than the standard Austin 7. The Swallow featured brightly colored aluminum panels, rather than the often black-painted fabric bodies of their rivals, and a polished radiator cowl that made owners feel that they weren't quite as badly off in a time of hardship.

When the larger Morris Cowley–based Swallow sold well, Lyons moved the business to a factory near Coventry to be closer to their suppliers. The company developed a range of other body styles, from sporting two-seaters to more luxurious drop-head saloons, and soon the profits started rolling in.

Lyons was ambitious, and in 1931 SS Cars Ltd. became manufacturers in their own right. Featuring a specially built chassis and a six-cylinder engine from Standard, the fixed-head coupe SSI captured buyers' imaginations with its rakish styling, superb build quality, and value for money. Though they were criticized for their poor performance, Lyons met that problem head on. He hired gas flow expert Harry Weslake and engineer William Heynes from Humber cars to improve the old Standard side-valve engine. The refined unit featured an overhead valve conversion, boosting power from 70 bhp to 105 bhp. For 1936, along with the new engine, a new name appeared for the range, echoing Lyons' predilection for animals renowned for their pace. The Jaguar was born.

Before the new engine was finished, the company released the stunning SS90, with its flowing fenders and long hood. Good for 90 miles per hour at only £395, it was an incredible value and laid the foundation for many Jaguar sports cars to come. With the new, more powerful engine, the model became the Jaguar SS100, one of the best-loved and most influential sports cars of the prewar period.

The war cut production short as the factory moved over to aircraft and prototyping work. But it was during this period that Heynes sketched out the initial designs for the brilliant XK engine that would define the postwar future for Jaguar for nearly 50 years.

When the war ended, the letters "SS" had been besmirched by the Nazis, so production resumed under the Jaguar name. Lyons appointed Lofty England as service manager. Wally Hassan, who had been hired just before the war, was R&D engineer. The sportier models had sold well abroad and Lyons managed to secure enough steel—which was rationed to companies that could secure valuable export orders—to continue the prewar models with a few updates. Jaguar also introduced the Mk V, a much roomier saloon but still with the pushrod engine.

The year that changed everything was 1948. As most British and European car manufacturers suffered under the postwar austerity measures, Jaguar launched the XK120 with the new twin overhead cam engine, independent front suspension, and sophistication and performance unseen before in a mass-produced automobile. With 120 miles per hour on tap, the XK was the fastest production car in the world. It was an immediate hit with the racing crowd on both sides of the

Atlantic, winning its debut race at Silverstone. Orders stacked up, necessitating the change from aluminum bodies to steel panels after just 200 units, and a move to the much larger former Daimler works in Browns Lane.

The XK's sweeping lines and blistering performance would lead Jaguar into one of the greatest decades for British motorsport. The 1950s would bring Le Mans successes for the C- and D-Types and witness the development of the most beautiful car in the world, the E-Type. Many great Jaguars would follow, from the sleek road-going saloons of the 1960s and 1970s to the further Le Mans

winners in 1988 and 1990—Tom Walkinshaw's fabulous XJR racers—to the remarkable supercars of the 1990s, the XJ220 and XJR-15. The company would suffer nationalization, nearly losing its identity under the British Leyland management, only to rise again after privatization with boosted investment during the Ford years.

Jaguar today is in good health with full-order books and a range of models that still reflects Lyons' core values of grace and pace, from the first SSI more than 80 years ago to the latest F-Type.

The Austin Seven, or "Baby Austin," was sold in hundreds of thousands in many guises, all featuring simple mechanics, a tiny four-cylinder lightweight engine with integral three-forward-speed gearbox, and a basic body shell. In the British market it nearly wiped out all other budget cars of its day, as the Ford Model T had done in the United States. However, it lacked sophistication and comfort. William Lyons recognized this and commissioned

AUSTIN SEVEN SWALLOW

Years of Production: 1927–1932
Engine: 747cc inline side-valve four-cylinder
Output: 7 horsepower
Top Speed: 48 miles per hour
Number Built: 3,500

master coachbuilder Cyril Holland to design a new, more elegant body. After a small-scale beginning, an order for 500 of Holland's variant

came through from London dealer Henlys in 1927. Swallow needed rapid expansion, including a move to larger premises in Coventry, to fulfill the order.

The Swallow bodies were clothed in aluminum panels over an ash frame and were very stylish, with plated round-nose radiators and bulbous tails. They proved to be highly distinctive in their two-tone color schemes and sold well in a time of austerity and global economic crisis.

1927 AUSTIN SEVEN SWALLOW

Where it all began for Jaguar: the SSI was an eye-catching sporting saloon, coupe, and tourer, and the first car to wear the SS badge. Lyons never clarified what the SS stood for—Standard Swallow, Swallow Sidecars, Swallow Special, or some other inspiration. Based on a special chassis built by Standard, the SSI drew much admiring press when launched at the London Motor show in 1931. It was also a tremendous value for the money at just £310. One of their advertising slogans keyed on this point, calling it 'The car with the £1,000 look.' Lyons penned the lines for the SSI and asked Standard to build a bespoke chassis for SS Cars Ltd. Standard would also supply running gear and engine for the new SSI.

Lyons wanted the car to be as low as possible, but his partner, William Walmsley, was concerned about headroom in the cabin. When Lyons was struck down with appendicitis during the vital design stages, Walmsley raised the roofline and the car. The result was fashionable at the time, but Lyons didn't like it.

The first chassis were overslung, with close-fitting helmet fenders, but after a production of

only about 500, SSI moved to an underslung chassis to improve looks and handling. The interior was sumptuous, with wood dash and leather bucket seats in the rear of the four-seat fixed-head coupe.

Although sporty in appearance with its long hood and racy marketing, the SSI lacked performance. It had only 48 bhp on tap and a top speed of 75 miles per hour. In 1934, there were larger engines with more power for the new saloon, and in 1935 Lyons corrected the gawky appearance with a gorgeous Airline coupe.

SSI

Years of production: 1931–1936
Engine: 2,054–2,663cc inline side-valve four-cylinder
Output: 48–62 horsepower
Top speed: 75 miles per hour
Number built: 4,254

Did You Know?

The early helmet-fender car was originally owned by an Italian princess.

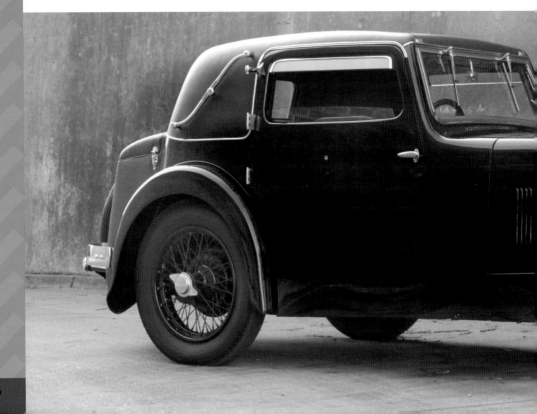

The SSI's little brother was ready for production in 1932, after a positive response at the 1931 London Motor Show. Demand for the two models was such that Lyons and his partner Walmsley ceased manufacture of the Swallow-bodied cars in 1933 and formed the SS Cars Ltd.

Initially launched with the 1,005cc Standard "little" Nine side-valve engine, the SSII looked fast but lacked power. It was capable of only 60 miles per hour, with its coachbuilt body and

SSII

Years of Production: 1932–1936
Engine: 1,005–1,608cc inline side-valve four-cylinder
Output: 38 horsepower
Top Speed: 60 miles per hour
Number Built: 1,792 in all models (FHC, saloon, four-seat tourer)

all-steel panels. The SSII was offered in fixed-head coupe, saloon, and tourer body styles, with chassis by Standard.

Horsepower improved for 1934, when the Standard 12 1,343cc and 1,608cc engine options were substituted, improving the little car's performance considerably. The later models also featured a four-speed synchromesh gearbox and servo-assisted brakes. The interior was sumptuous for a small car, with leather bucket seats in the back and a wooden dash with door cappings in an attractive cabinetmaker's finish.

The door panels themselves were works of art, with an Art Deco sun ray pattern shaped into the leather, and SS Cars purportedly used eight layers of paint in the finish. A Pytchley sliding roof was one of the more popular options, but in a market crowded with Riley, Triumph, and Hillman light cars all competing for the business, the SSII struggled to make its mark.

Did You Know?

The car shown here is one of just some 50 to survive.

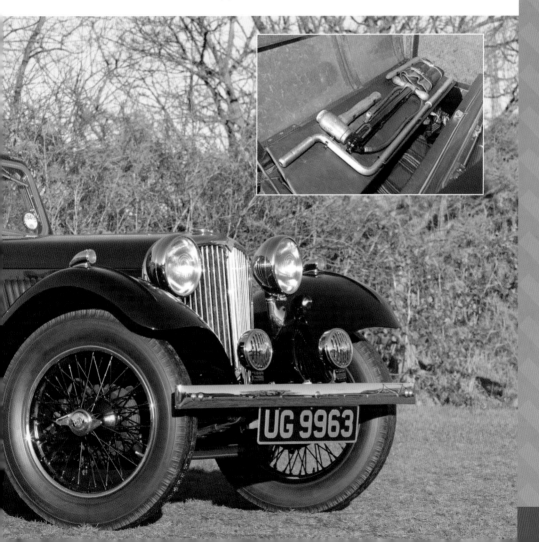

1936 SS100

Considered by many to be the world's first sports car, the Jaguar SS100 made its debut at the London Motor Show in 1936, initially with a 2.5-liter power unit. This was quickly upgraded to a new 3.5-liter inline-six engine. With a top speed of over 100 miles per hour, it could outperform virtually anything on the road, all for under £400.

Sir William Lyons used knowledge gained from building very aerodynamic motorcycle sidecars to come up with the sleek lines of the SS100. Despite being mocked by the purists of the day for their long showy fenders, cut-away doors, and folding windshields, SS100s were the chosen transport for those who loved great speed and rakish looks at the right price.

Competition successes in the RAC, Monte Carlo, and Alpine rallies were matched on the track by race ace Tommy Wisdom, who set fastest lap in an SS100 at 118 miles per hour to win the autumn handicap at Brooklands in 1937. It was this race-prepped, stripped-down model that truly put Jaguar on the map. The famous Jaguar "leaper" icon was first seen on an SS100. The first design of the Jaguar vehicle mascot was apparently described by the founder

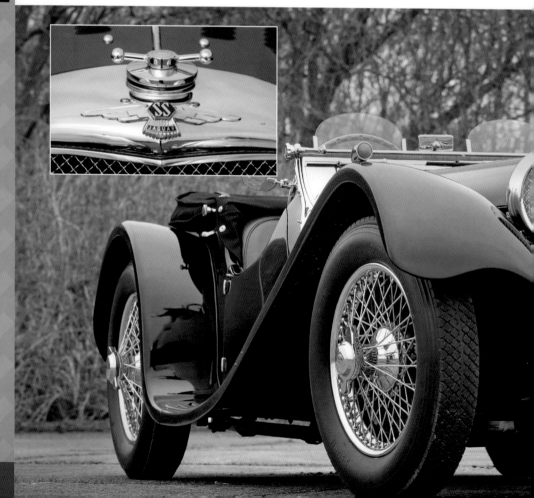

of the company as "looking like a cat shot off a fence." A later publicity photograph of the new Model 100 shows a revised Jaguar "leaper" mascot mounted on top of the radiator. Jaguar cars use that design to the present day.

The SS100 engine started out in 1936 at 2.5 liters, developed from the Standard unit. It was converted from side valve to overhead valve with a new cylinder head designed by engineers William Heynes and Harry Weslake. For 1937 it was enlarged to 3.5 liters, which delivered 125 horsepower through an excellent gearbox with synchromesh on three out of its four speeds.

When World War II broke out, SS100 production ceased, but Jaguar emerged from the conflict in fine fettle, building on its racing and engineering experience to produce a series of successful and popular sports cars.

SS100

Years of Production: 1936–1939
Engine: 2,663–3,485cc overhead-valve inline six-cylinder
Output: 125 horsepower
Top Speed: 104 miles per hour
Number Built: 314

Did You Know?

Harry Weslake, who designed the cylinder head for the SS100, would go on to design engines for Dan Gurney's famous Eagle-Weslake Formula One race car of the late 1960s.

Jaguar's first coupe concept was designed by William Lyons. *Autocar* magazine described its styling as "rakish and British" when the car was introduced at the 1938 London Motor Show. The SS100 Coupe was meant as a showstopper, and with no production models ready to launch, it appears that Lyons never intended to make any more than this one to promote the skill and styling behind the new Jaguar brand. Cyril Holland, master coachbuilder and freshly signing to SS cars, oversaw the hand building of the SS100 Coupe in Coventry. Featuring hand-beaten aluminum over an ash frame, the body was truly a one-off. The coupe shared only its hood and radiator with the roadster. Even the fuel tank was a larger one than fitted to the open cars.

Gone were the light, almost cycle-weight, fenders and running boards of the roadster, replaced with heavier flowing pontoon fenders and an unusual rear, lacking bumpers, to emphasize the tail styling. Due to all this extra bodywork, it was not unsurprising that the coupe was heavier by nearly 350 pounds than its open sibling, but it could still top 100 miles per hour, powered by the larger 3.5-liter Jaguar

straight-six overhead cam engine. In that rather bulbous tail, there was also a large trunk with the spare tire stowed underneath in a separate compartment. Under the hood, there was extra eye-catching brightwork so typical of the show cars, as well as paired inspection lamps to illuminate the engine bay.

The SS100 Coupe's lines presaged those of the superb fixed-head coupes to come, including the XK120 and E-Type. They also reflected Lyons' tastes of the day—he was particularly impressed with the flowing styling of the Bugatti Type 57S Atalante and smooth profile of the Alfa Romeo coupes. The one-off concept was the most expensive Jaguar the company had ever built at the time, at £595.

SS100 COUPE

Year of Production: 1938
Engine: 3,485cc overhead-valve inline six-cylinder
Output: 125 horsepower
Top Speed: 104 miles per hour
Number Built: 1

Did You Know?

The SS100 Coupe was sold off the stand to Leo March for his 17-year-old son, Gordon, who nicknamed the car "The Grey Lady."

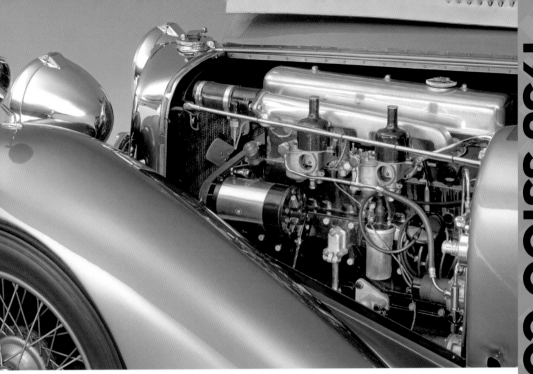

CHAPTER 1
POSTWAR: NEW BEGINNINGS

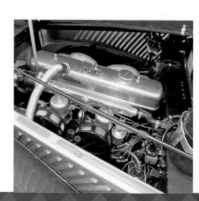

It's not often that a company, let alone an automobile manufacturer with such a complex product, gets a few years' break from production just to ponder what it will do in the future. But that's just what happened to Jaguar when World War II began in September 1939.

Building a range of models at their Coventry factory, including the racy SS100 sports car and 1.5-, 2.5-, and 3.5-liter saloon cars, it was still a young company before the war, with lots of ideas and the talented designers and engineers to make them a reality.

With the outbreak of hostilities, the factory was turned over to war work, specifically prototyping and aircraft fabrication. In an unusual twist, the factory took a step backward to restart building motorcycle sidecars. In fact, over the six years of war, they built more than 10,000 sidecars. They had again become useful for the military, and at the start of the war private citizens increased motorcycle use because of fuel rationing.

Also during that time, William Heynes, in discussion with Lyons, came up with the initial drawings for the engine that would carry Jaguar through the difficult postwar period and inspire a generation of future customers. Sticking with the straight six-cylinder configuration familiar from the SS100, Heynes realized that a twin overhead cam arrangement, although expensive to manufacture, would maximize efficiency and performance. This had been well proven in prewar racing machinery from Alfa Romeo and Bugatti, but the design wasn't commonly available in productions cars.

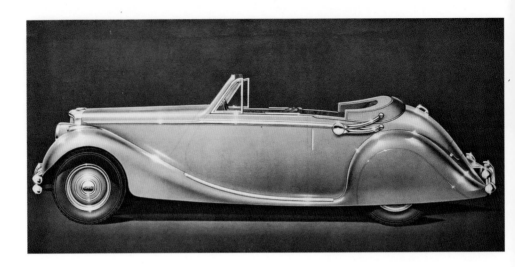

The engine that Heynes drew up during his many nights of fire watching on the factory roof was the now famous XK engine. It would become a reliable and flexible power source around which Jaguar could base its models for almost 50 years. This contribution should not be underestimated, for as other carmakers spent precious time and money developing numerous different powerplants for their cars, Jaguar's excellent XK unit was used in nearly everything. Sized from 2.4 liters to nearly twice that, the XK unit brought in economies of scale seldom seen in a production car. It was efficiency in production that Lyons had been so proud of before the war, and now he had the design for an engine with which he could take on the world.

Times were hard in 1945 when the newly named Jaguar car company got its factory back. Most materials were strictly rationed, particularly steel for manufacturing. It was available only to companies with a good record for export sales, to bring vital funds into Britain. Crucially, Jaguar cars had sold well in the United States in the years leading up to the war. Lyons was able to secure enough orders to allow him to get the prewar models, with a few modifications, back into production in under a year.

Lyons faced an agonizing couple of years tooling up for the new engine and planning the new 100-miles-per-hour saloon he had dreamt of building before the war. In the interim, he built a stop-gap model. It retained the pushrod straight-six engine but featured a voluptuous flowing new body. As with the previous models, it was tremendously popular and excellent value for the money, with its touches of elegant times past in a world starved of luxury.

As soon as the new engine was ready, it was rushed into production in a 3.4-liter version.

Lyons penned the lines of a svelte roadster to carry it. With little testing, it was introduced at the London Motor Show alongside the Mk V in 1948. The XK120 was the start of things to come and stole the show that year. Its name was derived from the top speed of 120 miles per hour, making it the fastest production car in the world at the time. The Mk V also proved a great success. Despite using rather old-fashioned technology, it did have independent front suspension, which improved the handling on such a large car.

It was the next big saloon that was to be the admiration of the world, bringing in an incredible $30 million of orders from the vital American market in the first few months. Named the Mk VII (Lyons didn't want to call it Mk VI because of the Bentley of the same name), it featured the new XK engine and boasted Lyons' much-dreamt-of 100-miles-per-hour top speed.

With the increased production demand, manufacturing moved to the old Daimler Browns Lane site in Coventry, where Jaguar still has a plant today. The Mk VIIM was introduced with 30 more bhp on tap, and a facelifted model called Mk VIII appeared in 1956.

Known for performance, Jaguar carried innovations proven on the track over to its road cars. One of the most significant technologies passed on to production models was disc brakes, used to such great effect by the D-Types at Le Mans. This advancement first appeared on all four wheels in servo-assisted form on the Mk IX, introduced in 1959. It was the first luxury production car to have them.

The days of the flowing bodywork on these luxury liners of the highway was coming to an end, and new fashions for more usable compact designs were on the horizon. Jaguar was ready.

Launched at the London Motor Show in 1948, the XK120 was originally created for a limited production run to stimulate interest in Jaguar after the war years and hopefully spark sales of the company's saloon models. But show visitors were bowled over by the sweeping lines and promised performance of the new William Lyons–designed car. Starved of motoring excitement since before the war, sporting drivers sent orders rolling in, and Jaguar happily changed its plans. The first 242 cars were hand-built with aluminum panels over ash frames until tooling was completed to

XK120 ROADSTER

Years of Production: 1948–1954
Engine: 3,442cc DOHC inline six-cylinder
Output: 160 horsepower
Top Speed: 120 miles per hour
Number Built: 9,400

make more economical pressed-steel bodies. Even then, the hood, trunk, and door panels remained aluminum.

The fabulous dual overhead cam straight-six engine was Jaguar's own design. It was not only strong—with seven main bearings—but also

powerful, delivering 160 horsepower, enough to propel the lightweight car to over 120 miles per hour. The top speed was respectable enough that Jaguar incorporated it into the XK's name. Competition success followed with a 1–2–3 finish at Silverstone in 1949. Later that year, Ian and Pat Appleyard famously won the Alpine rally in an XK120 registered as NUB 120.

A stunning coupe arrived in 1951, followed by a more luxurious drop-head coupe in 1953. The XK120's gearbox was a four-speed manual with synchromesh on the top three speeds. Suspension was independent at the front with wishbones and torsion bars, and a live rear axle and semi-elliptical springs for the rear. The Jaguar used hydraulically operated drum brakes all around.

Did You Know?

In May 1949, the XK120 was speed tested on the long Jabbeke straight in Belgium. With windshield removed, the sleek cat achieved a speed of 136.59 miles per hour, making it the fastest production car in the world at the time.

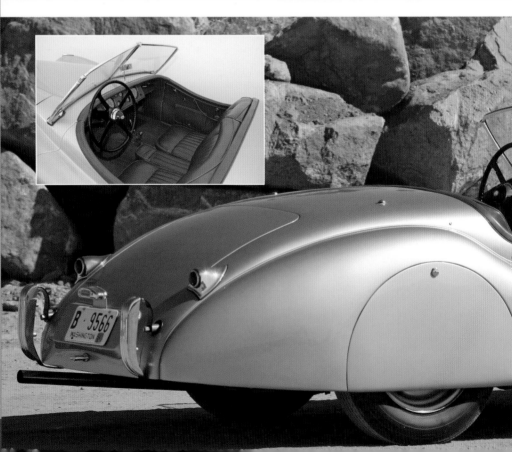

The Mk VII was the car William Lyons had staked the company on. It delivered with all the "grace, pace, and space" promoted in the brochures of the day. It was the successor to the Mk V, but Lyons didn't want confusion with the MK VI Bentley, so Jaguar skipped a mark and called its next model Mk VII.

Launched at the London Motor Show in 1950, and later the same year in New York, the Mk VII featured the straight-six XK engine developed by Heynes and Weslake and now well proven in the XK120 almost two years out of the stable.

With the US market in mind, Lyons designed the sweeping lines of the Mk VII by eye, helping his draftsmen and wood and clay model makers to realize the voluptuous coupe in three dimensions. Tooling up for the huge panels took longer than expected, and the car was delayed coming to the showroom. But it

was an immediate hit, with export sales of over $30 million in the first few months.

At more than two tons and sixteen feet long, it was a monster on narrow European roads. Yet with its luxury interior, smooth ride, and keen performance, the car sold well in the US, as hoped.

Despite their bulk, Mk VIIs were also popular and successful on the rally scene. In 1953, Ian Appleyard chose one for the 1953 Monte Carlo Rally and came within a second of winning, while Stirling Moss won the production car race at Silverstone in a Mk VII. The C-Types won at Le Mans the same year.

MK VII

Years of Production: 1950–1954
Engine: 3,442cc DOHC inline six-cylinder
Output: 160 horsepower
Top Speed: 103 miles per hour
Number Built: 20,908

Did You Know?

Jaguar introduced a Mk VIIM in 1954 to bridge the gap until the Mk VIII appeared in 1956. Courtesy of high-lift camshafts, the Mk VIIM made 190 bhp. More than 10,000 units were sold in 1954 and 1955.

The fixed-head coupe met public demand for a long-distance motoring sports car. The open cars were all well and good in California or on a British summer's day, but for much of the year they were a bit drafty in cold weather. Lyons was keen to broaden their appeal. With his experience producing the SS coupes before the war, William Lyons drew a gorgeous enclosed body echoing the lines of the new Mk VII saloon to complete the range of his already much admired XK120 sports cars.

The fixed-head coupe—Bill Heynes' own road car—proved itself in a demanding high-speed track test on the French Montlhéry circuit near Paris. Here, Leslie Johnson, Bert Hadley, Jack Fairman, and the young Stirling Moss drove the car for seven days and nights nonstop at an average speed in excess of 100 miles per hour.

The new fixed-head coupe was more luxurious than the earlier roadster version, if a little claustrophobic inside. Legroom was plentiful, however, with the seat mechanism effectively bolted straight to the floor. There were wind-up windows, exterior door handles, an abundance of leather, and a gorgeous

wooden dashboard with a large center-placed dial tachometer and speedometer. As in the roadster, the fantastic all-new overhead camshaft straight-six XK unit purred beneath the hood. The engine delivered up to 180 bhp with the special equipment package using high-lift cams and a higher compression cylinder head, or 160 bhp in standard form. There was enough power to propel the car beyond the advertised 120 miles-per-hour capability, but drivers had to be wary of the need to slow down again with only drum brakes at all four corners.

XK120 FIXED-HEAD COUPE

Years of Production: 1951–1954
Engine: 3,442cc DOHC inline six-cylinder
Output: 160–180 horsepower
Top Speed: 120 miles per hour
Number Built: 2,678

Did You Know?

During the Montlhéry speed trial, the car broke a suspension spring on the track's rough concrete surface when already well into the run. Leslie Johnson drove nine hours on the broken spring to maintain speed and spare the other drivers from added risk. When he finally stopped to have it replaced, the car had taken no less than five world speed records for a production car.

With the previous Mk IV models finishing production in 1949, Jaguar really needed a midsize saloon to fit between their large, luxurious Mk VII and the sporting XK models. Jaguar decided to use a unitary construction for the Mk I, a first for the company on a production road car. It took an investment of a million pounds, a huge sum in those days, to develop the model.

The D-Type racers used monocoque construction with tremendous success. Jaguar wanted to capitalize on the knowledge gained as well as the inherent rigidity, weight saving,

MK I

Years of Production: 1955–1959
Engine: 2,483–3,442cc DOHC inline six-cylinder
Output: 112–220 horsepower
Top Speed: 125 miles per hour
Number Built: 36,740

and handling benefits the design offered. The initial model was designed with economy in mind, featuring a detuned version of the six-cylinder overhead cam XK engine with a reduced capacity of 2.4 liters. The model's full potential emerged when the 3.4-liter power unit

was dropped in, making the Mk I one of the fastest saloon cars in the world.

Initial brakes were large drums, but as the top speed increased, Jaguar moved to disc brakes all round for later models. The full wheel spats fitted to the early cars were cut away to accommodate wire wheels with knock-off hubs. Mk I 3.4-liter saloons competed successfully in many rallies, touring car, and saloon car races. Notable drivers included Mike Hawthorn, Stirling Moss, and Roy Salvadori. The new body style remained in production in one form or another for nearly 15 years.

Did You Know?

The 1959 Formula One champion, Mike Hawthorn, was killed in a Jaguar Mk I just months after his retirement. He may have been street racing friend Peter Walker in a Mercedes 300SL at the time. It was just months after Hawthorn's retirement, and Lofty England, who had been Hawthorn race team manager and had loaned the car to Mike, had it destroyed.

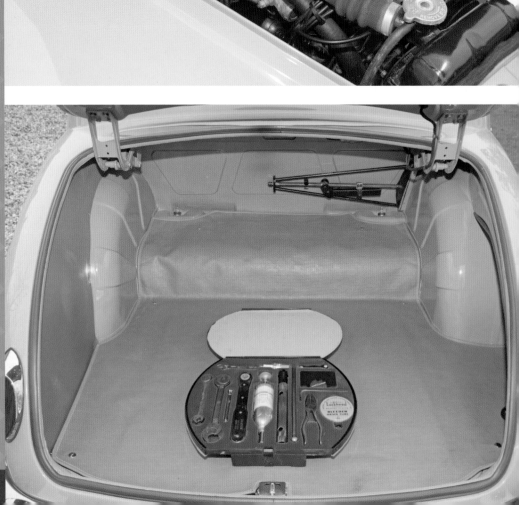

PSY·541

This was the last of the large, separate-chassis saloons that the Jaguar car company built. Fitted with servo-assisted disc brakes all round, recirculating ball power steering as standard, plus better performance from the larger 3.8-liter block—as would be fitted to the XK150S a year later—the Mk IX was one of the best cars of its day and Jaguar's flagship model. The Mk VIII had introduced the single-piece windshield, along with two-tone paint, and the two cars were very similar, with only minor

MK IX

Years of Production: 1958–1961
Engine: 3,781cc straight-six
Output: 220 bhp
Top Speed: 115 miles per hour
Number Built: 10,151

details, such as badges and taillights, differing in production. Transmissions were offered in four-speed manual, overdrive, and three-speed Borg Warner automatic featuring a rather

unsuccessful version of automatic brake called the Hill Holder, which frequently failed and was often disconnected. The interior was further upgraded with more leather and walnut and fold-away tray tables in the rear cabin, but it was already starting to feel a bit outdated.

With the Suez crisis, fuel prices had started to escalate and the time for outsized automobiles and sub-20-miles-per-gallon fuel economy was drawing to a close. Jaguar was focused on a new compact saloon.

Did You Know?

The Mk IX was highly popular as a ceremonial car for state dignitaries. When Charles de Gaulle made a state visit to Canada in 1960, the official cars for the motorcade were Mk IX Jaguars, rather than Cadillacs or Lincolns.

CHAPTER 2
BIRTH OF THE RACING LEGEND

Much of the legend we know of Jaguar today started with the new XK120 sports car launched at the London Motor Show in 1948. Racers were always on the lookout for the next car to beat their rivals, and the new XK fit the bill with its barchetta-style doors, lightweight construction, and powerful new engine. Being a Jaguar, the XK120 was also at the affordable end of the sports car market, with optional special equipment packages to increase power and stiffen the suspension. Racers made further changes, like swapping out the glass and metal windshield for aero-screens to reduce the weight, adding dual exhaust, and removing the wheel spats and fitting knock-off wheels.

The XK120 demonstrated its circuit racing prowess in 1949 when the Jabbeke speed trial car, converted to right-hand drive, won the Daily Express one-hour production car race at Silverstone with Leslie Johnson at the wheel, despite having a coming together with a Jowett Javelin.

In 1950, Johnson scored the first US win at a race in Palm Beach, Florida, and Phil Hill won his inaugural road races at Pebble Beach, California. These privateer victories convinced William Lyons that continued race success would be good for sales. He ordered the workshop to prepare six specially modified lightweight XK120s for the Le Mans 24-hour endurance race that year. Johnson and co-driver Bert Hadley did their best, holding second place for two hours at one point, but as the drum brakes faded they were left with no alternative but to use engine braking to slow down, which caused the clutch to fail. The remaining two cars finished in 12th and 15th places, giving the new XK120 worldwide recognition and foreshadowing increased prowess in the years ahead.

The XK120 in various specifications appeared in numerous races and rallies, including the Targa Florio, Mille Miglia, and Alpine Cup, where husband and wife team Ian and Pat Appleyard won the coveted Coupe des Alpes.

Along with the racing, Lyons entered XK120s in a number of high-speed record attempts. In 1951 Johnson and Stirling Moss achieved a remarkable average of 107 miles per hour over a 24-hour period, driving on the banked and bumpy Montlhéry circuit near Paris. The XK120 was the first production car to best 100 miles per hour average speed in one day—despite stops for tire changes and fuel. More records would follow, including one hour at over 130 miles per hour and seven days and nights at over 100 miles per hour.

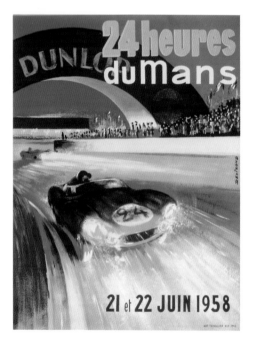

With these successes came headlines in the international press and tremendous advertising that money alone couldn't buy. Lyons, forever the businessman, knew he was onto something that fitted the Jaguar brand perfectly, and he was in exactly the right place to capitalize on it to improve sales of the road cars. Realizing that they had done as much as they could with the XK120 chassis and flowing body style, Lyons asked his competition manager, Lofty England, to press his engineers and designers to come up with a car for Le Mans the following year.

Starting from a clean sheet of paper, Bob Knight created a lightweight tubular space frame, which aerodynamicist Malcolm Sayer clothed in wind-dodging aluminum panels. The car was to be called the C-Type, or XK120-C in the US, featuring an uprated XK 3.4-liter power unit with more than 200 bhp on tap.

Three works cars went to the Circuit de la Sarthe in 1951. While two C-Types lost oil pressure and retired, the car driven by Peter Whitehead and Peter Walker came through to win, almost 10 laps ahead of the second-place Talbot. It broke the lap record in the process. The resulting chorus of praise for Jaguar was fantastic for the company, and Lyons became even more resolved to make competition a critical component of the marketing budget.

The C-Types did it again in style in 1953, finishing in first, second, and fourth. The newly developed disc brakes gave them a huge advantage in stopping power over the rival Ferraris and Aston Martins coming off the Mulsanne Straight. The winners were gentleman racers Tony Rolt and ex-RAF Spitfire pilot

JAGUAR

congratulate

Major A. P. R. Rolt and Mr. J. Duncan Hamilton
on their magnificent performance in the 1954

LE MANS

24 HEURES GRAND PRIX D'ENDURANCE

where they gained second place, following their great victory
last year when they set up a still unbeaten record for speed and
distance by achieving an average of 105.85 m.p.h. for 2540 miles

JAGUAR'S LE MANS ACHIEVEMENTS
1951 — 1st
1953 — 1st, 2nd and 4th
1954 — 2nd and 4th

LES 24 HEURES DU MANS 1952
PROGRAMME OFFICIEL
Prix : **200** francs

Duncan Hamilton, who had been disqualified by an officious ACO official during practice and had adjourned to the bar to drown their sorrows. Only after an appeal by Lofty England were they reinstated hours later and allowed to enter the race with, according to legend, more than a few drinks lightening their inhibitions.

For 1954 a new car was conceived, and this time it was to a monocoque, making it lighter and stronger for added stiffness under loading in the tight corners. A prototype was finished in 1953, and the new D-Types were on the grid at Le Mans the following year. A lack of competitive testing left all three cars suffering from fuel blockages early on, and although the fault was diagnosed and resolved, the drivers faced quite a battle to make up the lost time. Rolt and Hamilton finally roared back to finish in second place, just over a minute behind the winning Ferrari of Froilen Gonzalez and Maurice Trintignant.

The D-Type proved itself a few weeks later, winning the Reims 12-hour race with Ken Wharton and Peter Whitehead at the wheel. In 1955 the D-Type took the checkered flag at Le Mans with drivers Mike Hawthorn and Ivor Bueb, and in 1956 with Ecurie Ecosse privateers Ninian Sanderson and Ron Flockhart.

The1950s Jaguar Le Mans racing legend was further cemented the following year when D-Types took the first four places.

After the tremendous success of the XK120 at Le Mans in 1950, William Lyons was convinced that Jaguar should capitalize and build a special car for the 1951 race. In just over six months, they put together the XK120-C, or C-Type, as it was better known. Featuring more power, courtesy of a new high-compression head and bigger carburetors and exhaust, the new car was designed by aerodynamicist Malcolm Sayer and thoroughly wind tunnel tested. Weight loss was achieved by redesigning the chassis as a tubular space frame clothed

XK120-C/C-TYPE

Years of Production: 1951–1953
Engine: 3,442cc DOHC inline six-cylinder
Output: 210 horsepower
Top Speed: 144 miles per hour
Number Built: 53

in aluminum panels, while rack-and-pinion steering and torsion bar suspension improved high-speed handling.

The C-Type was an instant success, winning Le Mans in 1951 with Peter Whitehead and

Peter Walker taking the checkered flag. A lack of testing brought disappointment the following year, as all three C-Types overheated due to modifications made at the last minute. But C-Type drivers were on top of the podium in 1953, with Hamilton and Rolt busting the 100-miles-per-hour average for the first time in a new car featuring triple Weber carburetors and, for the first time, disc brakes. A limited production started in August 1952 and lasted about a year, with many of the 53 cars produced being shipped to the United States.

Did You Know?

The Jaguar C-Type competed in the 1952 Monaco Grand Prix in a year when F1 was in the doldrums. Tommy Wisdom picked up the car from Browns Lane and drove to Monaco, finishing sixth in the race behind five Ferraris. Stirling Moss would later win the Reims Grand Prix in the car the same year.

1951 XK120-C/C-TYPE

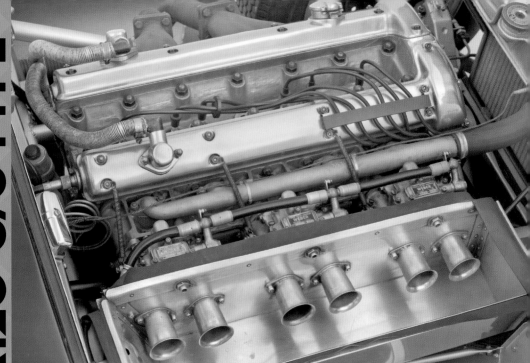

LSF 420

The C-Type had achieved about all it could do, with two Le Mans victories and even a Grand Prix first place, so Jaguar decided to start with a clean sheet of paper to design its successor, the D-Type. Malcolm Sayer, whose background had been with Bristol Aircraft, brought in aeronautical monocoque technology. The design featured a dry-sump engine, canted over to reduce overall frontal area, and that famous tailfin. There were also disc brakes all round, which were a necessity as the new car clocked 175 miles per hour on the Mulsanne Straight at Le Mans in 1954.

The Jaguar team, led by race manager Lofty England, was unlucky with fuel filter problems, however, and could only manage second place. They were back at Le Mans in 1955 with more power and long-nose bodywork, and despite the tragic crash when Pierre Levegh's Mercedes cartwheeled into the crowd, the D-Type driven by Hawthorn and Bueb went on to win. Only one of the three works cars finished at

Le Mans in 1956, but Jaguar was saved by privateer team Ecurie Ecosse, who won with drivers Sanderson and Flockhart. In 1957 the privateer Jaguars were unbeatable again and the first four places were taken by D-Types, with Flockhart and Bueb raising the trophy thanks to their 3.8-liter fuel-injected car.

But the days of a car built mainly to win one race were over, as Jaguar concentrated on filling its road car order books. It was the end of an era.

D-TYPE

Years of Production: 1954–1957
Engine: 3,42–3,781cc DOHC inline six-cylinder
Output: 275 horsepower
Top Speed: 175 miles per hour
Number Built: 42 to about 71

Did You Know?

In 1956 Jaguar became the first manufacturer ever to win both Le Mans with the D-Types and the Monte Carlo Rally, with the Mk VII, in the same year. It was also the year Sir William Lyons was knighted by the queen.

Jaguar released the XK140 as a roadster, fixed-head coupe with extended roofline, and drop-head coupe with two small extra seats in the rear. It felt considerably roomier than the rather claustrophobic XK120 coupe, with more interior space created by moving the engine bulkhead forward to give more legroom. A more powerful special equipment (SE) model featured an engine with the C-Type cylinder head, developing an extra 30 bhp, although all models still retained drum brakes all round.

XK140
Years of Production: 1954–1957
Engine: 3,442cc DOHC inline six-cylinder
Output: 190–210 horsepower
Top Speed: 125 miles per hour
Number Built: 8,984

Telescopic shock absorbers, rather than the old lever arm units, improved the ride and increased suspension travel, while rack-and-pinion steering made cornering more precise.

The XK140 was the first Jaguar sports car to be offered with the three-speed automatic gearbox. Standard steel wheel cars kept the spats of their predecessor, while the knock-off wire wheel option removed the spats and the heavier grille and bumpers. In recognition of the Jaguar racing success, there was a Le Mans winner badge on the trunk lid.

The roadster's interior was trimmed in leather and leatherette, including the dash, and a lightweight removable canvas roof worked with plastic side curtains. The coupe and drop-head coupe were more luxurious, with leather seats and walnut dash. As with the XK120, most were built in left-hand drive and exported to the United States.

Did You Know?

Italian dealer Guido Modiano commissioned coachbuilder Zagato to design and re-body his wrecked XK140SE. With the interior clothed in suede, it remains one of the few special-bodied Jaguars and was shown at the 1957 Paris Motor Show.

Like its predecessors, the XK150 was available in three body styles—roadster or open two-seater, as it was commonly termed (OTS); fixed-head coupe, which was as near as you could get to an XK saloon; and drop-head coupe. The facelift over the prior designs was striking, however. The fender line was straightened, raising the door and cowl height, and there was a wraparound one-piece windshield and full-width rear glass in the coupe. Thinner bulging doors with wind-up windows offered more interior space, and the dash was now leather-clad rather than

XK150

Years of Production: 1957–1961
Engine: 3,442–3,781cc DOHC inline six-cylinder
Output: 190–265 horsepower
Top Speed: 135 miles per hour
Number Built: 9,395

walnut. The lighting was upgraded too, with the addition of small repeaters on top of the headlights to show the driver they were working. Most cars were ordered with the Dunlop 12-inch disc brakes, which from 1958

were further improved to the quick-change brake pads developed for the D-Type racer.

There were the special equipment models, of course. The 150S delivered 250 bhp using the straight-port head and triple SU carburetors. When the 3.8-liter block was introduced in 1959, with the sport pack, power was boosted to a claimed 265 bhp. These most powerful engines, with higher compression, were denoted with gold paint, while less powerful versions were painted different colors depending on their reduced compression ratios of 8:1 or 7:1, for export to countries with poor-quality fuel.

The XK150 was a remarkable value at half the cost of its contemporaries with similar performance, such as the Aston Martin DB4 and Mercedes 300SL. With the arrival of the E-Type, the XKs were quickly considered old-fashioned and their values dropped like a stone. Many were driven into the ground, making original examples hard to find.

Did You Know?

Jaguar enthusiast Geoffrey Stevens built an XK150 shooting brake by welding the rear half of a Morris Minor Traveller onto the back of a very rusty coupe. The "Foxbat," as he named it, remains the only one in existence.

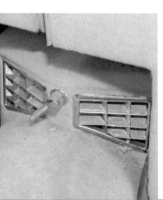

With Europe still struggling economically after the catastrophic war, William Lyons looked toward the United States for profits. Gasoline rationing wasn't completely lifted in the UK until 1950, five years after the war had ended, and manufacturing materials were strictly limited to those companies that could secure export orders. Jaguar, as SS Cars had become in 1945, was still a small company with only a limited range of models on its books in 1950, including the luxury saloon Mk V and exciting new XK120 sports car. But they were ahead of the game in the early 1950s compared to their rivals, as they proved on the track with wins from the XK120 and C-Types, and in road cars with their introduction of more modern luxury models Mk VII to Mk IX.

Lyons realized tremendous marketing advantage through racing, often at no cost to the company, as privateers scored success after success, including the final extraordinary result at Le Mans in 1957, when the first four cars home were Jaguar privateers. But Lyons saw at that time that the days of the gas-guzzling giant saloons such as Jaguar's Mk VII, VIII, and IX were coming to an end. Using technology derived through the racing program, Lyons and Jaguar started to develop a smaller executive-type saloon to be known as the Mk I to take the company into the new era. The Mk I was to be of monocoque construction like the D-Types, the first to be built for mass production, and involved a huge investment for new tooling and a manufacturing site.

Developments of the Mk I would carry the company from the 1950s through the 1960s and right on into the 1970s with the Mk II, S-Type, and 420. On the track, these smaller sporting saloons were popular with the racers, who succeeded with the Mk I and later with the more powerful Mk II, driven by the likes of Stirling Moss, Jim Clark, and Mike Hawthorn. Rallying successes were gained in the Tulip Rally in 1958 plus team prizes and class wins in the Monte Carlo, RAC, and Alpine Rallies. Jaguar saw five successive victories in the increasingly tough Tour de France. The 1963 event, marking Jaguar's last victory, consisted of 3,600 miles of high-speed motoring. On the road, the flagship Mk X would evolve from these slant-fronted designs without losing the luxurious touches so reminiscent of a past decade. This evolution of both styling and engineering had been one of the great strengths of Jaguar over the many years of the company.

The
4·2 LITRE MARK TEN JAGUAR

There were also new models on the sporting side, targeted directly at the US market. The sleek XK140 and XK150 used more powerful versions of the fantastic twin cam engines to boost performance beyond 130 miles per hour and disc brakes developed from the racing program to help them stop.

William Lyons practiced economies of scale, and this prudence had carried the business through difficult times in the past. Now as Jaguar moved into mass production, it was again to become essential. The new XK power unit was the proof of all that Lyons held dear—a single engine that was so flexible, it could be used in capacities from 2.4 to 4.2 liters, serving every production model and reducing overheads significantly in comparison with the other automobile manufacturers of the day. For many years, Jaguar had been Britain's top dollar earner and the most popular imported car in the United States.

With the Mk I saloon nearing five years of production, the Mk II arrived with a number of improvements. A wider rear track enhanced handling in corners, and there was more glass all round to help visibility, as the engineers realized that the roof pillars could be narrowed without loss of rigidity. The larger 3.8-liter engine was now also an option, and with more torque it worked better with the automatic transmission fitted to most cars exported to the United States. These cars also featured a limited slip differential to avoid tail wagging under hard cornering

MK II

Years of Production: 1959–1967
Engine: 2,483–3,781cc inline six-cylinder
Output: 120–220 horsepower
Top Speed: 125 miles per hour
Number Built: 83,976

at speed. Power steering was also an option, introducing the light-touch characteristics that would epitomize the later saloons.

The Mk II proved a popular and successful race and rally car. Many future champions cut

their teeth driving this nimble and fast saloon, including Bruce McLaren, Graham Hill, and John Surtees. Wire wheels assisted cooling on the hard-pressed disc brakes, particularly when racing. The Mk II's impressive performance also made it the preferred choice for many criminals. To catch 'em, the police ordered a number of cars with low back axle ratios for metropolitan use and in 3.8-liter spec for the newly opened British motorways, which at the time had no speed limit. Final incarnations appeared in 1967, called the 240 and 340. There was also a Daimler-badged version with a superb V-8 engine after Jaguar had acquired the company in 1960.

Did You Know?

A Mk II Jaguar in the hands of French drivers Bernard Consten and Jacque Renel achieved tremendous road rally results, winning the grueling Tour de France for the fourth time in successive years in 1963 over a course of 3,600 miles.

The new flagship model introduced in 1963 was the Mk X. It bore little resemblance to its immediate ancestor the Mk IX, as the engineers had done away with chassis and separate body construction and moved to a monocoque design. Built with the US market in mind, the new car featured the 3.8-liter XK engine and a widened version of the independent rear suspension seen on the E-Type. It was a giant at almost 17 feet long and more than six feet wide, but was no slouch. It could propel five passengers to a top speed of 120 miles per hour

MK X AND 420G

Years of Production: 1961–1970
Engine: 3,781–4,235cc inline six-cylinder
Output: 220–265 horsepower
Top Speed: 120 miles per hour
Number Built: 24,282

in great comfort when the larger 4.2-liter engine was fitted in 1964. Luxury fittings included a fold-out rear picnic table and a front-seat pull-out picnic table stowed beneath the instrument cluster. Later, air conditioning and a soundproof

glass division between the front and rear seats were added as options. The appeal was certainly strong in the United States and Canada, where orders were in excess of $60 million, but it wasn't as successful in Europe, where the roads were more narrow.

In 1966 the Mk X was renamed the 420G at the London Motor Show, identified now by a central bar in the radiator grille, side indicator repeaters, and a chrome strip down the side. Two-tone versions were available but lacked the chrome strip. Inside were a few safety changes, including a padded edge to the dash. There was also an equivalent Daimler named the Sovereign to add to the range, but this was mostly badge engineering of the 420G.

Did You Know?
The Daimler DS 420 Limousine, which was based on the Mk X floorpan and hand-built by Jaguar, was used extensively as official state cars by the British, Danish, and Swedish royal houses.

The 420 was apparently introduced on the express insistence of William Lyons, who disliked the rather ugly lines of the S-Type and was disappointed with sales of the flagship Mk X model. Costing only £200 more than the S-Type, the 420 was more equivalent to its luxurious big brother than the 420G, having been developed from the Mk X. With many styling cues penned for the forthcoming XJ6, the new car featured a totally redesigned front end with slanting forward grille with four headlights and flatter tops to the fenders, reflecting what was to come next. There were

420

Years of Production: 1966–1970
Engine: 4,235cc inline six-cylinder
Output: 245 horsepower
Top Speed: 124 miles per hour
Number Built: 10,236

also narrower straight bumpers side to side without the central dip of the Mk II and S-Type, making the car look much more modern. The cabin was very well appointed with armrests for the front- and rear-seat passengers, and now a padded dash and door capping to keep up with

new safety laws. The larger 4.2-liter XK engine was in twin SU carburetor spec and faster than its predecessor with only 20 bhp less power on tap than a contemporary E-Type. It also handled considerably better, with an upgraded version of their independent rear suspension and limited slip differential. There were options for variable ratio Marles Varamatic power-assisted steering, offering very light feel straight ahead but quickness into the corners, and a choice of transmissions, including overdrive on the manual cars. A dual-circuit hydraulic brake system replaced the single-circuit system in the S-Type with discs on all wheels. Other improvements introduced on the 420 included an alternator instead of dynamo, larger cross-flow radiator, and negative ground.

A Daimler model named the Sovereign was also introduced, but the nameplate was the biggest difference from the Jaguar car.

Did You Know?

The car shown was exported to South Africa in 1967 in CKD form . . . that is, Completely Knocked Down to its barest essentials and built upon arrival. This included a special headlining in vinyl instead of cloth, specific for the South African cars.

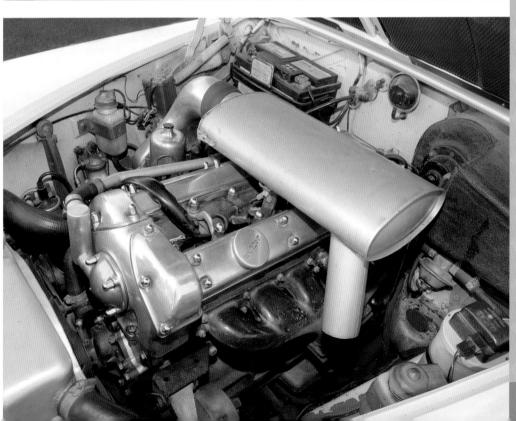

CHAPTER 4
THE MOST BEAUTIFUL CAR IN THE WORLD

If a single car can define a company, then for Jaguar it has to be the E-Type.

It epitomizes all that William Lyons held true, born from the latest designs and engineering proved on the racetrack and evolving into a market-leading sports car so much admired around the world. A bit like Elvis or Coca-Cola, the E-Type is a universal icon loved by all those who have a passion for automobiles and appreciate what is behind the sleek lines and impressive performance. It was one of the first cars that created a lifestyle rather than aspiring to it. If you were lucky enough to own an E-Type, passersby gawked and other motorists got out of the way to get a better look at who was behind the wheel. From the earliest Series I in 1961 to the final black-painted V-12, the long hood and throaty roar of the E-Type became part of the patchwork of our lives, adding color and excitement to a rather drab period in British motoring.

One of the E-Type's strengths—and there were many, from the cutting-edge suspension geometry to the road-hugging five-inch ground clearance that remained with every model—was its sleek and slippery shape, penned by Malcolm Sayer, the aerodynamicist whose early aircraft career would influence so many Jaguar models. The E-Type's design was like nothing else on the road at the time, quite a leap of faith for the company and in stark contrast to the cars of today with their homogenous CAD styling. The long hood harked back to the prewar SSI, which, although looking fast, wasn't, but still did the trick for sales. The engine, Jaguar's near-perfect XK unit, already 13 years old when the E-Type came out, carried the sports car to nearly 150 miles per hour in its 4.2-liter form. The cutting-edge monocoque body was augmented with a tubular subframe at the front, and there was independent suspension and disc brakes all round, something virtually unheard of in the early 1960s on any car, let alone one that cost £1,600 when launched in 1961.

As predicted by the press, the E-Type was an immediate sales success both in roadster and fixed-head coupe forms, especially in Jaguar's main export market, the USA. Like the XK120, it also won its first race outing, at Oulton Park in April 1961, with driver Graham Hill seeing off competition from Innes Ireland in an Aston Martin DB4GT. Although it was the spawn of the

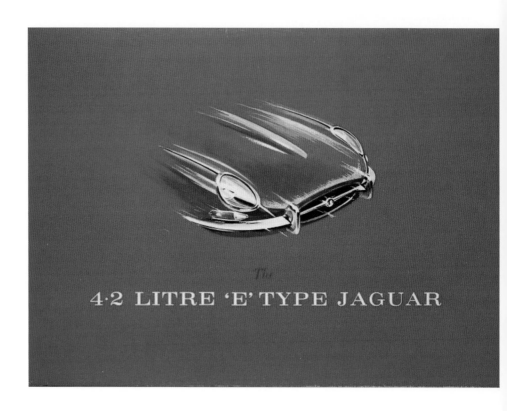

The
4·2 LITRE 'E' TYPE JAGUAR

pure race bred D-Type, it was the racer for the masses, opening doors for many great drivers to enter the rarified motor sports world in both lightweight and standard cars. British ace Roy Salvadori and American Briggs Cunningham took fourth in an E-Type in their first try at Le Mans in 1962, and the car evolved with a number of more and more extreme racing developments, such as the low-drag coupe. It became the staple sports racer on the American scene, where Merle Brennan proved almost unbeatable in the Sports Car Club of America series from 1962 to 1964. It improved as it matured with a larger engine, and the death knell was finally called not because of poor sales but due to Ralph Nader and his safety campaigns in the early 1970s.

Jaguar V-12:
The ultimate cat

The missing-link car between the racing D-Type and the road-going E-Type is a prototype called E2A. Much more than the usual dummy bodywork, it cobbled together mechanicals of many development models of the day.

William Lyons was very keen to capitalize on the great competition success of the 1950s with no less than five Le Mans wins during the decade. He also wanted to recoup some of the company investment by building a road car and include many of the cutting-edge technologies developed by the racing program. So in February 1960, E2A was wheeled out from the Browns

E2A E-TYPE PROTOTYPE

Year of Production: 1960
Engine: 2,997cc DOHC inline six-cylinder
Output: 300 horsepower
Top Speed: 135 miles per hour
Number Built: 1

Lane experimental workshop. With its tailfinned rear bodywork, it recalled the D-Type, but that's where the similarity ended. The one-piece front bodywork hinted at the gorgeous lines of the forthcoming E-Type. The new E2A was to test several features of the forthcoming production

model, not least its independent rear suspension system featuring a simple Heynes design using four coil spring shock absorbers and lower wishbones with the driveshafts forming the top suspension link.

There was also an all-new semi-monocoque chassis design with inboard disc brakes at the rear to reduce unsprung weight and deliver better handling. E2A was powered by an aluminum-block Lucas fuel-injected 3.0-liter XK engine, later uprated to a larger 3.8-liter block and carburetors for SCCA racing. It was subsequently delivered to the Cunningham team in their famous American racing colors, white overall with two parallel center-line stripes in dark blue, and entered in the 1960 Le Mans race with Dan Gurney and Walter Hansgen at the wheel. Although one of the fastest cars down the Mulsanne Straight, it suffered an oil pipe failure and had to retire.

Did You Know?

Many other famous drivers drove E2A, including Bruce McLaren and Formula One world champion Sir Jack Brabham.

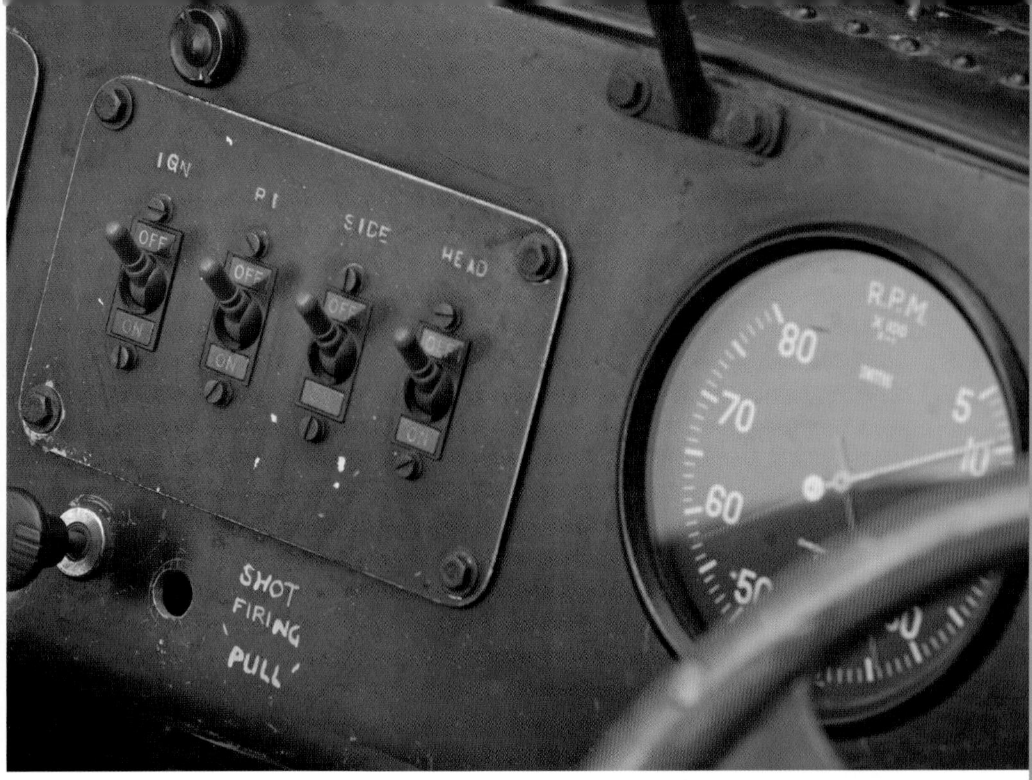
IGN
P.I
SIDE
HEAD
OFF
ON
SHOT
FIRING
PULL
R.P.M.
X 100
80
70
60
5

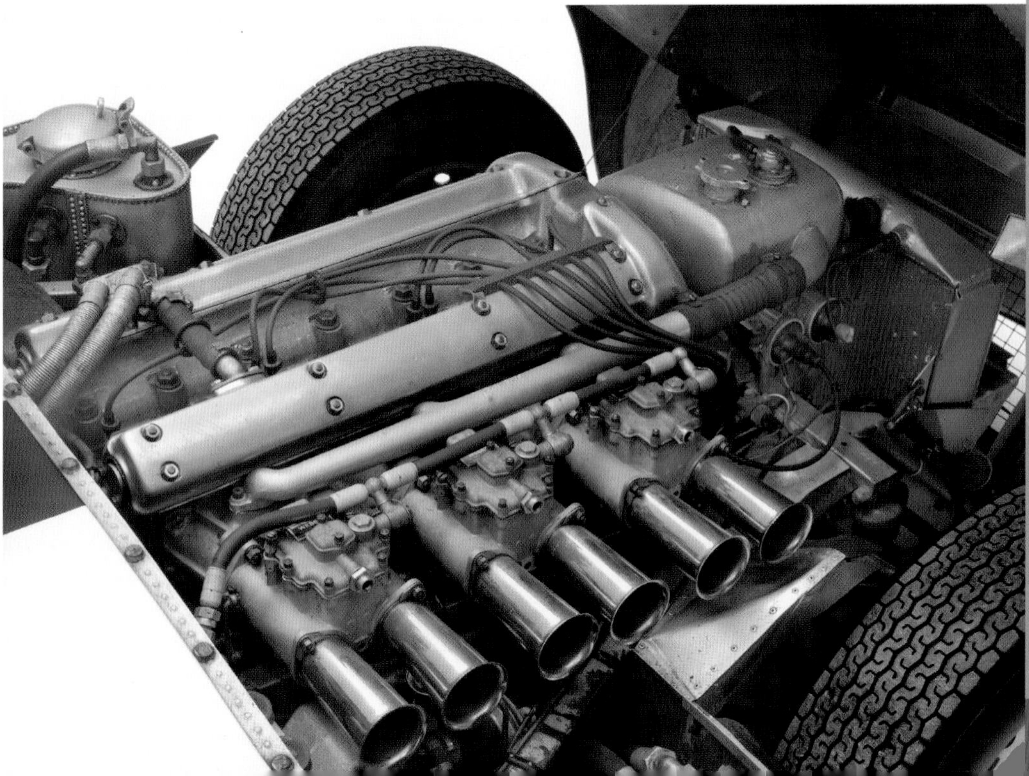

Unveiled in 1961 to great fanfare—Enzo Ferrari himself is reported to have said that the new car was "the most beautiful car ever made"—the Jaguar E-Type is one of the world's most recognizable sports cars. Its stunning shape came from the pen of aerodynamicist Malcolm Sayer, who was given free rein to design the most streamlined monocoque body the wind tunnel could deliver. It featured independent rear suspension with coil springs and a torsion bar on the front end, coupled with a low ground clearance of just five inches. Although steering

E-TYPE (XKE) SERIES I AND II

Years of Production: 1961–1970
Engine: 3,781–4,235cc DOHC inline six-cylinder
Output: 265 horsepower (six-cylinder)
Top Speed: 150 miles per hour
Number Built: 57,230

lacked precision in the earlier iterations, Jaguar soon addressed the problem with a rack-and-pinion system. There were also all-around disc brakes as standard now, as well as inboard configuration at the rear to reduce unsprung weight and improve handling.

When it first went on sale, Jaguar struggled to keep up with demand, as it was priced at just £1,600 with 150 miles per hour on tap. Under its long hood was the 13-year-old XK block bored out to 3.8 liters. While well-proven in the C-Types and D-Types, the motor had become a bit dated. It was replaced by the better 4.2-liter version, with a much stronger bottom end, in October 1964, coupled to an all-new gearbox.

A whole range of models (named XKE for the US market) arrived, including a two-plus-two (which was longer by nine inches with more headroom), two-seater coupes, and the famed roadster. The coupes used one of the first hatchback rear doors. For the Series II E-Type in 1968, Jaguar introduced open headlights and a collapsible steering column to keep up with the latest safety trends in the US, as well as bigger bumpers. There was also an intermediate model Series I ½, which is very desirable without the larger bumpers.

Did You Know?

In 1962 Lew Grade wanted to borrow an E-Type for Roger Moore to drive in his new hit show, *The Saint*, but Jaguar turned him down as they were selling every car they could build.

The "Lightweight" E-Type was intended as a follow-up to the D-Type. Jaguar had planned to produce 18 units, but ultimately only a dozen were reportedly built, using a fully alloy monocoque clothed in riveted aluminum panels to form a stressed skin. The first car, later called the Low Drag Coupe, was effectively a Jaguar development car designed by Malcolm Sayer. It included a lower windshield and a more pronounced slope with the rear hatchback welded shut for rigidity. The interior trim was discarded with only insulation around the transmission tunnel, and there were rear brake

E-TYPE LIGHTWEIGHT

Years of Production: 1963–1964
Engine: 3,841cc DOHC inline six-cylinder
Output: 300 horsepower
Top Speed: 170 miles per hour
Number Built: 12

cooling ducts on the rear wheel arches. With the exception of the windshield, all cockpit glass was perspex. A tuned version of the 3.8-liter engine with a D-Type wide-angle cylinder head made it really quick. Although the low-drag coupe, now with registration CUT 7, suffered

from overheating, it still managed to beat a bunch of 250 GTOs in the support race for the 1962 Reims Grand Prix with Dick Protheroe at the wheel.

From this early car, the factory Lightweight E-Types evolved, but all were built as roadsters. Many raced with bolted-on hardtops, however, and a few cars were rebodied into low-drag coupe form. Briggs Cunningham took his Lightweight E to Le Mans in 1962 and finished fourth overall. The cars featured many modifications, including triple 45DCO3 Weber carburetors, although some racers ran with fuel injection.

Another race car with a rich history is the Lindner Nocker car, built up in low drag spec with the most powerful engine ever fitted to a Lightweight E-Type, with 344 bhp on tap. It was virtually destroyed at the French banked circuit of Montlhéry, but has recently been painstakingly restored.

Did You Know?

Two research engineers at London's Imperial College, Samir Klat and Harry Watson, applied their cutting-edge knowledge to another Lightweight E, raced by Peter Lumsden and Peter Sargent. Among other modifications, it featured a longer nose reminiscent of the Vanwalls.

1963 E-TYPE LIGHTWEIGHT

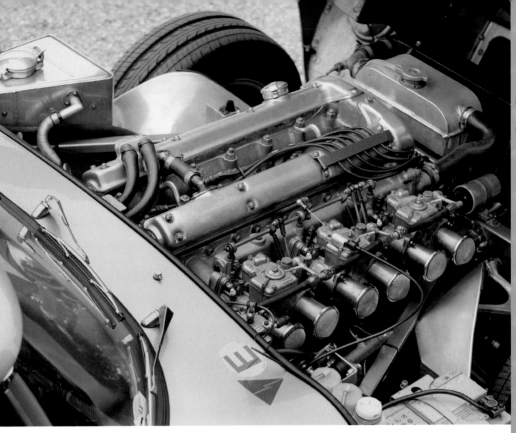

In 1971 a brand new 5.3-liter V-12 Jaguar engine, with an alloy cylinder block derived from the long-dead XJ13 project, was shoehorned into the E-Type and called the Series III. It marked the first volume production V-12 since Lincoln's in 1948. The lighter block, although physically bigger, produced an engine of similar weight to its precursor, yielding handling characteristics similar to the previous series. While it lacked some of the subtleties of the first cars in looks, the new beefed-up E-Type,

E-TYPE (XKE) SERIES III V-12

Years of Production: 1971–1975
Engine: 5,343cc DOHC V-12
Output: 272 horsepower (V-12)
Top Speed: 150 miles per hour
Number Built: 15,287

sporting wide arches, big tires, and a grille in the radiator aperture, was a hit all over again. Updates included power steering, ventilated disc brakes, and an early form of Lucas-Opus

electronic ignition with Zenith carburetors. The new ignition restored some of the performance lost to the US-led emission controls, which were starting to choke the older XK engine.

The Series III was built as the standard two-door roadster as well as a two-plus-two version in coupe form on the longer-wheelbase floorpan. Sales dipped toward the end and Jaguar struggled to sell the last few E-Types—an ignominious end to a legendary sports car.

Did You Know?

The last special-edition E-Types, 50 roadsters in funeral black with hardtops, rolled off the production line in Coventry in 1974—a final bow for a legendary player in sports car history.

1974 E-TYPE (XKE) SERIES III V-12

The Eagle Speedster is a modern take on the E-Type built by specialist E-Type restorer and race engineering company Eagle, which is based in the rolling countryside of East Sussex in England. The first Speedster was built as a special commission for an American client, who requested something even more special than their "usual" bespoke Jaguar E-Type roadsters uprated for current-day use.

Although initially a one-off, Eagle had such great interest in the Speedster that they decided to build several more. There will only ever be a very limited number due to the small size of the company, and they will be all-aluminum, hand-built special commissions, each built to order.

The process begins with an original Series I Jaguar E-Type. Although the transformation is dramatic, Eagle claims the Speedster remains

a genuine Jaguar E-Type under its new slippery skin. The donor car receives electronic ignition, a modern electronic fuel pump conversion, and an uprated cooling system with improved fans and custom wiring with reliable modern switching. Eagle improves brakes and enhances handling with Koni shock absorbers and wider six-inch wheels with modern tires. The car gets a stainless-steel exhaust system as well as enhanced heating and demisting. More powerful headlights complete the initial "basic" specification.

The most noticeable design detail is the seamless flush body, hand-crafted in aluminum across its contours and the track, which is extended with widened wheel arches. The sills are lowered to give it the Speedster look, and there are aluminum-rimmed wheels with knock-off spinners. The car retains the same E-Type headlight and taillamp style and oval radiator opening so familiar from the original car.

Under the hood is Eagle's own all-aluminum 4.7-liter XK engine with speed-sensitive electric power-assisted steering, five-speed gearbox, fuel injection, and even a recirculating air conditioning system. Inside the cockpit there is aluminum, lots of leather, a cleverly concealed handbrake in the armrest, and a fabulous view down the long hood through the lowered and raked windshields.

EAGLE E-TYPE SPEEDSTER
Years of Production: 2011–2015
Engine: 4,694cc DOHC inline six-cylinder
Output: 310 horsepower
Top Speed: 160+ miles per hour
Number Built: 4

Did You Know?
Eagle has also built its very own take on the Low Drag GT. It offers the same power-to-weight ratio as a new Porsche 911 Turbo.

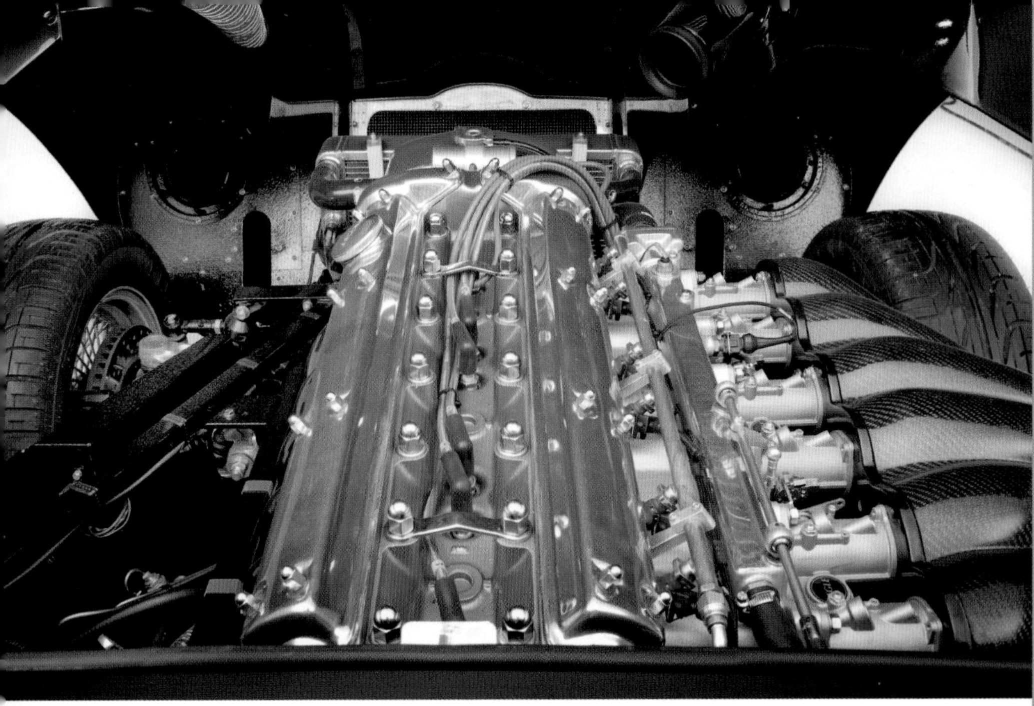

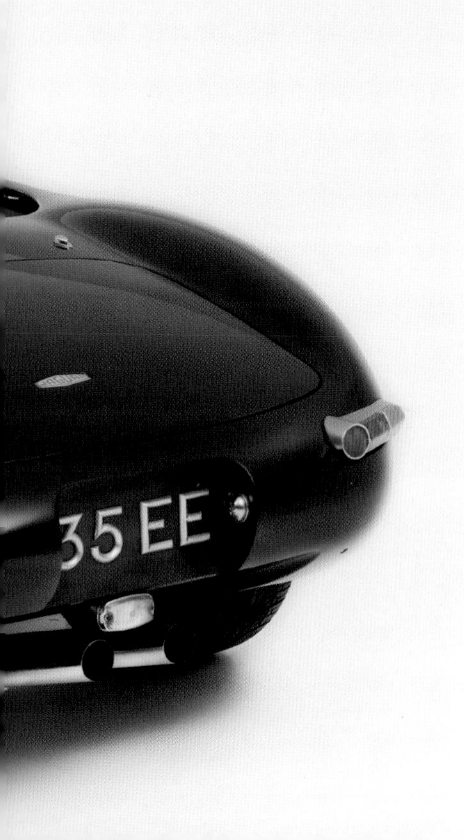
35 EE

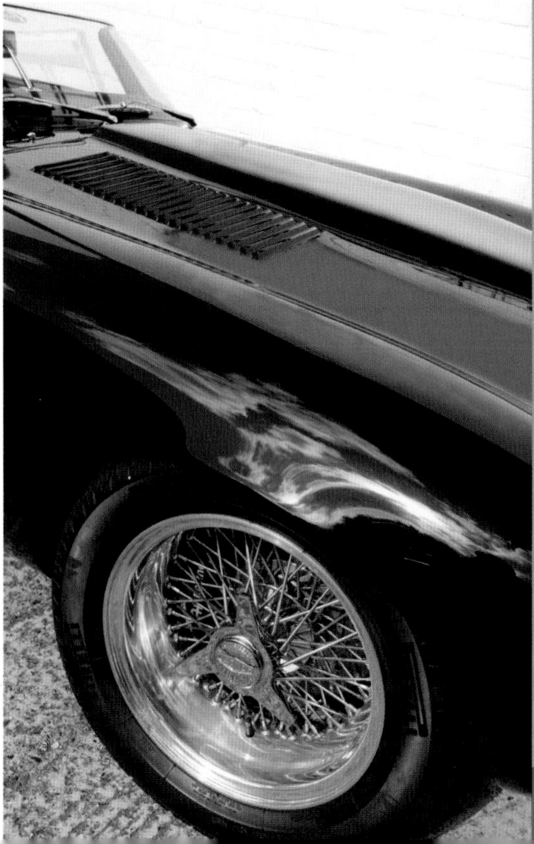

In 2014 Jaguar announced that it would build six new Lightweight E-Types to complete the series of 18 cars that was started in 1963, of which only 12 were originally built. Original examples are now valued in the many millions. The most desirable of all the E-Types will be manufactured in aluminum to the exact specifications of the original cars, and assigned the six remaining chassis numbers that were originally allocated.

The Lightweight carried approximately 114 kilograms (250 pounds) less weight than a standard E-Type, thanks to its all-aluminum body and engine block, a lack of interior trim and exterior chrome work, and a host of further weight-saving features, including lightweight,

hand-operated side windows. Using state-of-the-art scanning technology, the inner and outer surfaces of a Lightweight body shell were digitally mapped to redraw accurate plans for the new cars.

The monocoque body shell was built at Whitley, where it was mated to its tubular engine subframe—which is stiffened for the original Lightweight—and then shipped to Jaguar's Gaydon facility for painting. From there, it was taken to Jaguar Heritage at Browns Lane special operations department, where the car was built up with powertrain, suspension, brakes, steering, electrical items, instrument panel, and soft trim. The lucky chosen customers will also be able to make

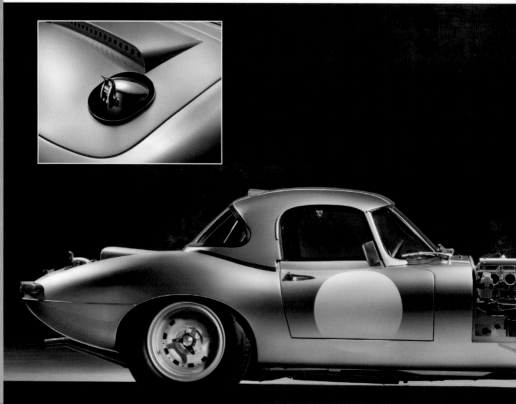

special requests for interior and exterior trim levels, paint and livery, and further technical specification.

Even the same type of Connolly leather will be used, with hides produced to the same specification as those used by Jaguar in the 1960s. This leather is used to trim the competition-type aluminum bucket seat base.

The competition wheels were made from a magnesium alloy to save weight. Suspension and rack-and-pinion steering remain as in the first batch, with independent wishbones on the rear, set up according to period racing practice with uprated shock absorbers controlling the torsion bar springs on the front and the four coil springs on the rear.

The six-cylinder XK engine mirrored the original power units, with an aluminum block and steel cylinder liners, bored out to 3.8 liters, rather than the cast-iron block used in the road cars. It also featured a dry-sump lubrication system, as in the race cars, with scavenge pump recirculating the oil at high pressure. A big-valve, wide-angle cylinder head, and 10:1 high-compression pistons enhanced power. Customers had the choice of three 45DCO3 Weber carburetors, or Lucas fuel injection, as with the first cars.

The cars were sold as period competition vehicles, and all are suitable for FIA homologation for historic motor sport purposes. As with the original cars, an aluminum hardtop was standard.

Reviving the Lightweights was a nod to Lyons and his understanding that racing prowess and commercial success were intertwined. These special cars reflect well on the current F-Type and XJ models, also being built to exacting standards with aluminum bodies.

LIGHTWEIGHT E-TYPE

Years of Production: 2014–2015
Engine: 3,841cc
Output: 340 horsepower
Top Speed: 170 miles per hour
Number Built: 6

Did You Know?

There will actually be seven new Lightweight E-Types built, not six. Car Zero, according to Jaguar, is effectively an engineering prototype and will not carry one of the six Lightweight chassis numbers.

CHAPTER 5
GRACE, PACE, AND SPACE

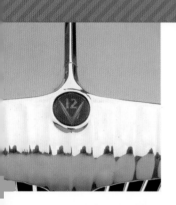

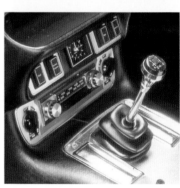

Jaguar had merged with Daimler in 1960 and eventually sold out to British Motor Company (BMC) in 1966. BMC in turn was amalgamated into British Leyland in 1968. It was an imperfect environment to introduce the pinnacle of William Lyons' idea of a sporting saloon, but in 1968 the fantastic XJ6 made its appearance. The timing was right, as the company had a confusing range of saloons in a variety of shapes and sizes on the market, from the smaller Mk II executive saloon to the leviathan Mk X. Penned by Lyons himself, the new XJ6 not only looked superb, but thanks to Bob Knight's sterling work on chassis development, the car also set new standards of ride and refinement. The styling, particularly at the front end, was an evolution from the 420, with its flat, low radiator grille and four-headlight presentation.

With the arrival of the XJ saloons, all other saloon models were deleted with the exception of the 420G, which continued until 1970 with just a handful of cars leaving the factory. To satisfy a larger spread of the market with just one body style, Jaguar offered a choice of the familiar 4.2-liter XK engine or a new 2.8-liter variation introduced with an eye on the European market, where there were strict tax restrictions on the larger-engined vehicles. The majority were sold with the 4.2 engine. The price, at just under £2,253, as ever was quite remarkable, and the waiting lists were long. Jaguar officials were so confident about the identity of the new car that they placed no name badges on the bodywork, just that Big Cat leaping on the sills and on the grille.

The Series III V-12 E-Type was still selling well, particularly in the US, so Lyons decided to create the ultimate luxury sporting saloon by fitting the V-12 engine into the XJ chassis. The resulting XJ12 had more than 250 bhp on tap. This five-seater brought out in 1972 could top 150 miles per hour, but yielded 12 miles per gallon of fuel.

The two XJ6 engines were developments of the fabulous XK unit. The 2.8-liter unit was squarer in design and more free revving. Featuring the traditional twin-SU carburetors and straight-port cylinder head, it delivered a healthy 180 bhp and a top speed of 118 miles per hour. Lyons understood his market. He knew the 2.8 model would sell in the thousands to top-notch salesmen, the 4.2-liter model to management, and the Daimler version to directors, covering the whole business car sector.

There were serious build-quality issues under British Leyland, with rust a common problem. Jaguar had to fight to maintain its identity and funding among the larger group of car manufacturers, but the XJ6 and XJ12 were good products and they sold like hotcakes. The engineers had been so successful in

keeping down the road noise—largely thanks to rubber-mounting everything—that the XJ6 was the first road car to use Dunlop's new low-profile radial tires, which enhanced road holding and handling enormously. In 1970 Jaguar was building 650 XJ6s a week, with 100 going straight away to fulfill orders in the United States. Assembly of the now outdated 420G saloon was stopped to make way for increased production at Browns Lane.

To compete with Mercedes, Jaguar offered a long-wheelbase version with four inches of additional legroom in the rear cabin. An "L" was added to the badging for these cars.

The poorly selling 2.8-liter model was dropped in 1973, and the facelifted Series II came out in the same year, introduced at the Frankfurt Motor Show. With United States sales an important part of the order book, there were stiff crash regulations to comply with, meaning a higher front bumper. The company took the opportunity to modernize the interior, too, particularly the dash. Instruments in front of the driver were redesigned.

European Touring Car Championship 1984 JAGUAR

The year 1973 also marked the final project that Sir William Lyons worked on, the XJC or coupe version of the XJ6. Using the short wheelbase chassis and longer front doors, the car had a striking pillarless profile, but it caused the engineers no end of headaches with wind noise and leaking door seals. Due to these issues, the car didn't appear in showrooms until 1975. A limited number of road cars were fitted with the V-12, and the tuning firm Broadspeed campaigned a team of XJ12Cs in the British touring car championship of 1977.

The XJS went on sale in April 1975 as successor to the E-Type, which was ceased the same year. Lasting for more than 20 years, it went through numerous specification changes and engine options, but never quite lived up to its stylish predecessor.

In 1980 Jaguar was re-privatized, allowing it once again to plow its own furrow. One of the immediate improvements was build quality, sorted out after agreement with the unions about their assured future with the company. A new, more fuel-efficient six-cylinder engine breathed life into the XJS in 1983 and XJ6 in 1986. It featured a 24-valve cylinder head, and although it had less power at 228 bhp, it offered better acceleration due to its reduced weight.

William Lyons' styling at its best. The public got a sneak preview of the look to come on the underrated stop-gap 420 model, released at the end of 1966, two years before the XJ6 launch. With its slant-front radiator grille and quad headlights, it was very modern-looking and continued the Jaguar philosophy of grace, pace, and space perfectly. The ride was second to none, thanks to superbly conceived all-independent suspension, including anti-dive

XJ6 SERIES I

Years of Production: 1968–1973
Engine: 2,792–4,235cc DOHC inline six-cylinder
Output: 180–220 horsepower
Top Speed: 118–150 miles per hour
Number Built: 78,218

geometry, and a smooth-delivering rubber-mounted engine for a feeling of peace and well-being behind the wheel.

Although two engine capacities were available, 2.8 and 4.2 liter, most sales came from the large-block model, as the smaller unit suffered from overheating and poor performance figures. The 4.2 was good for 120 miles per hour with five passengers on board, and it could stop, too, with four-wheel discs. Inside it was pure luxury, with leather everywhere and gauges mounted in front of the driver rather than centrally in the wooden dashboard. The XJ6 in one form or another would remain recognizable in the Jaguar range for almost 40 years, a grand legacy to the man whose final great project it became.

Did You Know?

The XJ6 was voted Car of the Year in 1969 by a panel of motoring journalists, amid abundant media praise.

Appearing four years after the XJ6, the XJ12 was a car to make any gearhead's heart beat a little faster. It featured Jaguar's brand-new all-alloy 5.3-liter V-12 engine squeezed into the very same engine bay that took the straight-six. Unsurprisingly, the performance for such a saloon was blistering, with a top speed of more than 150 miles per hour in sensational comfort and silence for the driver plus four passengers on board. In the pre-energy crisis days, its 12 miles to the gallon consumption was not unusual. Fuel economy improved somewhat when the Series II was introduced in 1975, with fuel injection instead of four carburetors. The SII V-12 was now only available on the long-wheelbase floor plan, and with the fuel injection came a boost in

power to 285 bhp. This jumped further to 299 bhp when the HE (high-efficiency) head came along with the SIII in 1981. A truly fantastic sporting saloon, it paved the way for more of the same in the years ahead. As with its little brother, it remained in production for decades, once again proving that Lyons' economies-of-scale approach was a good one.

XJ12

Years of Production: 1972–1992
Engine: 5,343cc V-12
Output: 253–299 horsepower
Top Speed: 150 miles per hour
Number Built: 27,961

Did You Know?

The Daimler version of the XJ12, the Double Six, was voted "The Best Car in the World" by motoring journalists when it debuted.

The Series I was a hard act to follow, but as times were changing, the XJ6 had to evolve along with them. The usual health and safety updates were necessary to enable sales in the US, which Jaguar managed better than most other automobile manufacturers of the day. A higher front bumper and crash zones in the cabin barely changed the look from the 1968

XJ6 SERIES II/III

Years of Production: 1972–1988
Engine: 2,792–3,442–4,235cc DOHC inline six-cylinder
Output: 162–235–251 horsepower
Top Speed: 123 miles per hour
Number Built: 199,452

original. The most striking visual difference was a shallower radiator grille, which along with the raised bumper line caused the hood to appear lower, giving the Series II a sportier look. There was a midrange 3.4-liter engine added in spring of 1975, with 162 bhp on tap, and the smaller 2.8-liter unit built mainly for export to Europe, where stringent taxes hit bigger-engined cars.

Pininfarina facelifted the Series III, introduced in 1979, with a flatter roof, larger windows, and restyled nose. The old XK engine was finally dropped in 1986, in favor of the new AJ6 24-valve unit as already featured in the XJS. The new powerplant boosted performance to 235 bhp, and improved economy with the 4.0-liter option.

Did You Know?

A Jaguar Sport XJR was introduced in 1988 to give the model its final true incarnation. Rated at 143 miles per hour at the top end, it was the fastest XJ6 built.

The grand tourer XJS was introduced to the buying public in April 1975, having been on the drawing board as successor to the E-Type since the late 1960s. Brought in to compete with the Lamborghini and Ferrari V-12 GTs on the market at the time, it bore little resemblance to the E-Type. It was based on a shortened version of the XJ floor plan and launched with a 285-bhp 5.3-liter V-12 power unit that propelled it to over 150 miles per hour. Due to concerns from the United States about the safety of open-top cars, the XJS was initially designed as a

XJS

Years of Production: 1975–1996
Engines: 3,590cc DOHC six-cylinder, 5,343–5,993cc V-12
Output: 228–304 horsepower
Top Speed: 123–158 miles per hour
Number Built: 145,490

two-plus-two coupe. It later appeared as a Targa top and eventually as a cabriolet, but it was not until 1988 that common sense prevailed among the health and safety brigade and a full

convertible arrived. An unusual buttress affair stood out in the styling at the rear and those heavy safety bumpers dominated the front, as demanded by US campaigners such as Ralph Nader. A smaller-engined version, using the all-new AJ6 3,590cc straight-six 24-valve power unit, was introduced in 1983 to counter the gas-guzzling argument. Buyers responded well, purchasing more than 90,000 of the model by the time it was dropped in 1991. With only 228 bhp available and a manual gearbox, it gave better acceleration than the V-12 and with fewer visits to the fuel pump. The ultimate incarnation of the XJS appeared in 1992, when engine capacity climbed to 6.0 liters, making over 300 bhp. The last XJS rolled off the Browns Lane production line in 1996.

Did You Know?

Bob Tullius won the 1977 American Trans-Am series by racing a production V-12 XJS for the famous green-and-white liveried Group 44 Team.

Some of the most exciting and sexiest Jaguars ever built have been unintended consequences of racing projects or never-built concepts punching way above their weight in the history books.

Circumstance and opportunity have often been a large part of these special projects, such as the glorious XKSS born from the 1950s endurance racing program. It now seems hard to believe that there were a number of unsold D-Types lying around the competition department, and when William Lyons heard about this he tasked his designers and engineers to convert them to road-going cars with the minimal budget available. What transpired was to become one of the most iconic and valuable cars Jaguar ever produced, with only 16 completed before a fire that destroyed a number of unfinished cars at the factory in Coventry. Owners now can name their price, and there's no sense knocking if your first number doesn't have six or seven zeroes behind it.

With so much of the Jaguar brand resting on its incredible motor sport reputation, it seems remarkable that there are not more of their stillborn ex-racing prototypes around. The truth is that racing is a very expensive endeavor. So Jaguar carefully pursued motor sports in short bursts, as with Le Mans in the 1950s and at the end of the 1980s. They could then exploit the kudos to market the road cars while barely tinkering around the edges of racing, relying on privateers to campaign their cars and continue the good press and PR with no further company funds. This clever strategy has kept the Jaguar name out there on the racing scene for nearly 70 years, with the minimum of works team sponsorship.

There have been a few blips in the otherwise near-perfect competition history. One of these, the XJ13, never actually raced at all due to the complicated politics of the time. The mid-engined design by Malcolm Sayer had been conceived to take on the mighty Ford GT40s and Ferraris at Le Mans, but its development and testing got held up during wrangling between the top brass, as Jaguar was taken over by BMC. Sufficient funding to perfect the design was hard to come by. By the time it was ready, it was already obsolete and would have been a mere footnote in Jaguar's racing history had it not been for the spectacular accident the XJ13 was involved in on a press day in front of the cameras five years later. The crash nearly destroyed the car. Fortunately the wreck wasn't scrapped, but tucked away and later rebuilt. It regularly appears at motoring festivals all over the world—a stunning one-off that missed its chance.

No less remarkable, the XJ220 fortunately emerged to become one of the greatest and fastest supercars on the planet. Incredibly, it started out as a pet project by enthusiastic Jaguar designers and engineers who were underwhelmed by the run-of-the-mill cars they were working on at the end of the 1980s. Rather than sacking or reprimanding their inspired designers, Jaguar took the XJ220 at stunning face value and introduced the design as a concept car. The motoring press went nuts for it and customers put in orders.

Bringing the concept to production took longer than hoped, and a global economic crisis left Jaguar with another expensive, unsold stock. Slightly overlooked at the time, although a contemporary to the XJ220, is the lesser-known XJR-15 developed by TWR from the racing XJR-9 Le Mans–winning chassis. More than 50 of these fabulous cars were built, which with 450 bhp on tap were capable of nearly 200 miles per hour.

The one thing all of these Jaguars have in common is that the company took a loss on them.

The XKSS is one of the fastest, most beautiful, and most valuable road-going cars Jaguar ever made, yet its genesis is something of a mystery. One explanation is simply that Jaguar was left with 26 unsold D-Types and William Lyons told his engineers to build them up into road cars; they were then fitted with XK140 rear lights, windshields, headlight cowls, and a passenger door. Another story is that works racer and Le Mans winner Duncan Hamilton had modified his race car to road-going spec and that that vehicle inspired the XKSS. Either way, very few would deny that the D-Type-derived XKSS is one of the greatest sports cars ever built and, due to a fire at the factory in Browns Lane that destroyed a number of the unfinished cars, one of the rarest.

With race car performance and a slippery shape designed in the wind tunnel by Malcolm Sayer, it was powered by the XK engine in

dry-sump form. The combination was enough for an eye-watering speed of over 150 miles per hour—not bad for the 1950s. It featured a magnesium alloy body over a monocoque center and tail, bolted to a multi-tubular steel front frame that supported the engine as in the D-Type. There was a rudimentary convertible top for weather protection and thin chromed bumpers split either side, front and rear, a styling cue that would later reappear on the E-Type.

XKSS

Year of Production: 1957
Engine: 3,442cc DOHC inline six-cylinder
Output: 250 horsepower
Top Speed: 150 miles per hour
Number Built: 16

Did You Know?

Steve McQueen's favorite car was a Jaguar XKSS, which he loved so much that after selling it in 1969 he rebought it in 1977. He once escaped a speeding ticket in the car by pretending that his pregnant wife, Neile, was in labor.

Jaguar's thoughts had often turned to competition, reflecting on their decade of Le Mans wins in the 1950s. In 1964, a small team including Malcolm Sayer and Mike Kimberley, later to head up Lotus cars, convinced Jaguar that they could take on the GT40s and Ferrari if they built a mid-engined car. So as part of their new engine program, William Heynes decided to design a completely new power unit—a marriage of two XK sixes with the familiar double overhead cam top ends joined onto a new lightweight aluminum block, creating a quad cam 4,994cc 60-degree V-12.

XJ13

Year of Production: 1966
Engine: 4,994cc V-12 quad cam
Output: 502 horsepower
Top Speed: 175 miles per hour
Number Built: 1

The new V-12's development went in two directions, road and racing, with six SU carburetors for the street and Lucas mechanical fuel injection for competition. The new car, now named XJ13, was penned by Sayer and built in great secrecy in 1966. It

was based on the D-Type monocoque, with wide sills to accommodate fuel tanks that minimized problems with front to rear weight distribution. Power ran through a five-speed transaxle ZF gearbox.

The V-12 engines were fitted to three Mk Xs for testing, but the XJ13 itself got delayed due to Jaguar's amalgamation with the British Motor Corporation and didn't run until 1967. Although tested on the track by ex-Jaguar apprentices and race drivers David Hobbs and Richard Attwood, the prototype never turned a wheel in a race. Ford by then had developed the seven-liter GT40 update, effectively rendering the XJ13 obsolete. It was brought out in 1971 for a promotional day at the MIRA test track, but driver Norman Dewis lost control on the banking at high speed after a tire blowout and the car was badly damaged.

Did You Know?

The wrecked XJ13 was hidden away in a shed at Jaguar for many years but eventually rebuilt to run at historic demonstrations. Factory test driver Norman Dewis was finally able to take the wheel again for a guest appearance in 2006.

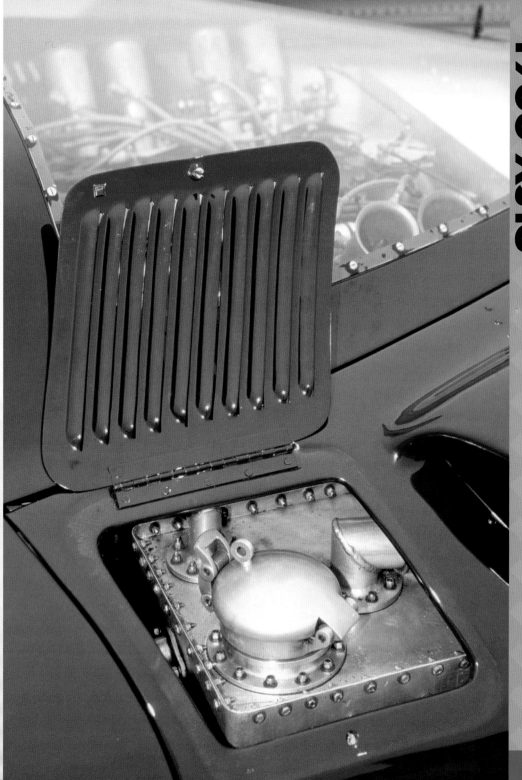

Tom Walkinshaw conceived the road-going XJR-15, based on the 1988 Le Mans–winning XJR-9LM. He brought in Peter Stevens to sculpt fresh lines for it. The new car was to be the world's first fully composite, carbon fiber, and Kevlar road-going car. It would feature the same central monocoque as the Tony Southgate–designed XJR-9, with a 6.0-liter normally aspirated lightweight race-derived V-12 engine mounted centrally. It weighed about the same as a contemporary

XJR-15

Years of Production: 1990–1992
Engine: 5,993cc V-12 cylinder
Output: 450 horsepower
Top Speed: 191 miles per hour
Number Built: 53

VW Golf, but had 450 bhp on tap for 0–60 in a staggering 3.9 seconds. It was built by Jaguar Sport, a partnership of Jaguar and TWR at their Bloxham works in Oxfordshire.

The car used a five- or non-synchromesh six-speed manual transaxle gearbox, Zytek engine management system, and fly-by-wire throttle, which was highly advanced for the time. The cockpit, functionally cramped on the race car, was widened and the headroom lifted. Bumpers, lighting, and a spoiler were added, but little more was done by way of comfort. Gearshift was on the right and the steering wheel cut away at the base to allow better access. The race cars were designed with a low ride height to make the most of the underfloor aerodynamics, but this was raised on the road cars for practical reasons and it had little effect on their handling at legal speeds. Five cars were produced using the large 7.2-liter Le Mans engine as used in the race version.

Did You Know?
The XJR-15 featured in a one-make racing series called the Jaguar Intercontinental Challenge, which supported three Formula One races (Monaco, Silverstone, and Spa) in 1991 with a winner of the final race to take a $1 million prize.

The incredible XJ220 project was dreamt up by a group of Jaguar engineers in their spare time. They called themselves "The Saturday Club," and led by Jim Randle, they proposed to build the ultimate supercar. It was started in secret at Jaguar's Whitley engineering plant in the Midlands, and the plans took a huge leap forward when management discovered it and showed the car at the 1988 London Motor Show as an official concept. The car's reception was tremendously positive, and in the buoyant economic climate of the day, Jaguar was persuaded to take it into production.

XJ220

Years of Production: 1992–1994
Engine: 3,498cc twin-turbo V-6 cylinder
Output: 500 horsepower
Top Speed: 220 miles per hour
Number Built: 275

The original design featured a V-12 engine mounted amidships and four-wheel drive, but this proved too bulky. A twin-turbocharged quad cam V-6 and rear-wheel drive replaced it, a decision that would come back to bite Jaguar. The power was still impressive with the

smaller engine. With four valves per cylinder, twin fuel injectors, and dry-sump lubrication, the howling V-6 delivered 500 bhp and brutal acceleration of 0–60 in 3.5 seconds. The XJ220 was listed as the fastest production car in 1992.

The expansive body—nearly five meters long and more than two meters wide—was designed by Keith Helfet and built using an aerospace-type bonded aluminum honeycomb chassis inspired by the Group C race cars. Tom Walkinshaw, with his race car experience, was entrusted to build 350 XJ220s at a brand-new facility in Oxfordshire, and the order books looked full. But as a financial downturn evolved, many prospective buyers sought to back out of the deal. Many customers took legal action to retrieve their £50,000 deposits, citing the V-6 replacement engine and switch from four-wheel drive as the deal-breaker. The XJ220 was initially successful in GT racing, winning its class at Le Mans in 1993, but it couldn't compete with the McLaren F1 when it appeared on the scene.

Did You Know?

The list price for an XJ220 was a stiff £403,000 when it went on sale in 1992 ($678,000). A couple years later, you could pick one up for a fraction of that price.

After Jaguar closed its works sports car competition department in 1956, it was more than 25 years before another company-sponsored race car would turn a wheel again in anger. John Egan was keen to build a sporting performance reputation again when he became chairman in 1980. He called on veteran racer Bob Tullius in the United States to plan a strategy. Tullius had successfully campaigned a Series III E-Type and an XJS V-12 in the Trans Am series and would now add the might of the Group 44 team to create an endurance race car.

Beginning with a North American racing program, the plan centered on building a prototype to meet both IMSA GTP and FIA World Endurance Manufacturer's Championship rulebooks. The result was this car, the 1982 XJR-5. Lee Dykstra designed the XJR-5's chassis and aerodynamics, creating a smoothly contoured and aggressive shape and taking full advantage of the long and narrow Jaguar V-12 engine to accommodate large ground effects tunnels for down force. The XJR-5 was otherwise quite conventional— an aluminum tub, Kevlar composite body panels around the Jaguar 6.0-liter V-12 with six dual-throat Weber carburetors supplying enough of go juice to make over 600 bhp.

The result, although fairly simple, was effective, and the XJR-5, co-driven by Tullius and Bill Adams, showed its potential immediately with a third place overall and first in GTP at Road America in August 1982, and then a first overall at Road Atlanta and second at Laguna Seca in 1983.

Successive XJR-5 racers were built, competing in both the IMSA and FIA series, including the 1984 24 Hours of Le Mans, where drivers Tullius, Brian Redman, and Doc Bundy failed to finish. The following year, though, they were back and came in 13th overall behind a field almost exclusively of Porsches and took the class win.

This success whetted Jaguar's appetite. They engaged Tom Walkinshaw to create a new prototype in the World Endurance Championship and at Le Mans the following year, while Group 44 continued focusing on IMSA in the United States.

The new XJR-6 used the normally aspirated Jaguar V-12, as in the old car, but Formula One designer Tony Southgate created a brand-new carbon fiber tub to take on the Porsches at their own game. Sadly it wasn't meant to be, despite minor successes. It would take a further three years, as the Jaguar evolved through XJR-7, -8, and -9, before Porsche's stranglehold on the series could be broken.

In 1988, TWR entered a pair of the new XJR-9s in IMSA spec for the Daytona 24 Hours. The cars, sponsored by Castrol and finished in a very smart green, red, and white livery, achieved victory at their first event. At Le Mans in June, there were four XJR-9s, but two quickly failed due to gearbox problems. The race was exceedingly close, with the Jaguar of Johnny Dumfries, Andy Wallace, and Jan Lammers in the lead, and the Porsche 962 of Derek Bell, Hans Stuck, and Klaus Ludwig shadowing right behind in second place. Wallace had probably never driven a racing car at 200 miles per hour before, certainly not for longer than a few moments, and he was awed to realize that his XJR-9 was covering the Mulsanne Straight at a full 240 miles

per hour, which was 10 miles per hour faster than his elders had been going 12 months before. The Jaguars were extremely fast and handled a lot better than the previous year's XJR-8LM, and given the necessary reliability they were bound to equal, or exceed, the performance of the three works Porsches. After 23 hours, Jan Lammers heard an ominous clunk from his own gearbox, but by holding the gearlever in fourth gear he managed to remain in the lead for the final 40 minutes, taking the checkered flag with Ludwig hot on his heels just over a minute behind. Jaguar was the Le Mans winner again after more than three decades!

For 1989 there were two all-new cars designed by TWR for IMSA and Group C racing, the Jaguars XJR-10 and XJR-11. Both cars featured a smaller turbocharged V-6 engine. They fared rather better in the IMSA series than the World Series, with two of the new XJR-9s fitted with the larger V-12s taking the first two places in the classic Daytona event. The same winning package was slotted in for Le Mans, as the smaller V-6s lacked the staying power for endurance contests. During the race, the Jaguar struggled to fourth at the finish line, behind a 962 and a pair of Sauber-Mercedes. It was the last time the Mulsanne Straight would be tackled without chicanes, as the cars were nearing speeds of 250 miles per hour.

Tony Southgate's final race chassis for Jaguar was to be the 1990 XJR-12.

It reverted to the 7.0-liter V-12, and again two of the XJR-12s were entered for the famous 24-hour Florida classic at Daytona. At the finish the winning Jaguar, driven by US star Davy Jones, Jan Lammers, and Andy Wallace, was four laps ahead of the other Jaguar, which finished in second place.

At Le Mans that year, the XJR-12s proved quick in practice. This time the Jaguars hung back at the start of the race, and during the afternoon allowed the unreliable Nissans, Toyotas, and Mazdas to fall by the wayside. Martin Brundle in the number one car had a nasty moment when the windshield broke and the engine suffered a water leak during the night. It was the car that wasn't to last, being retired around dawn. The other three TWR XJR-12s were doing well, and Walkinshaw, realizing that Jaguar could win, wanted a Brit on the winning team, so he switched Brundle into the number three car, ousting a highly disgruntled Eliseo Salazar in the process. At the line, it was Jaguar's turn again at last to top the podium, with the number two car coming in right behind, ahead of a Porsche 962C.

Crowds, mostly British, packed the circuit for the presentations, drunk with enthusiasm for a seventh Jaguar win. Perhaps it was fitting that having started the "new" generation of Jaguar racing, the winning car should be an IMSA-based XJR-9, converted to XJR-12LM spec in the UK.

While 1990 marked the last Le Mans win for Jaguar, it also saw Jaguar regain the World Sports Car Championship with the revolutionary XJR-14 totally dominating the series, including the Le Mans 24-hour race. Despite narrowly missing out on victory, Jaguar recorded one of its greatest Le Mans results in 1991, with three V-12-engined XJR-12s finishing second, third, and fourth.

William Lyons would have been very proud of the most successful racing Jaguar since the D-Type. It was an evolution of racing technology years in the making, with success along the way as with its predecessor, the C-Type.

The TWR XJR-12LM race winner was actually built in September 1987 as an XJR-9, chassis number 288. In preparation for a life in the States as an IMSA entrant, it was given a shakedown at Donington by TWR driver John Watson. Finished in Castrol livery, it was initially fitted with the six-liter version of the V-12 engine good for 650 bhp, and sent

over to compete in the 1988 season. Just three Castrol-sponsored XJRs were entered. It was to be TWR's first attempt at Daytona, and after qualifying sixth, the team won the grueling 24-hour event with drivers Martin Brundle, Raul Boesel, John Nielsen, and Jan Lammers.

The XJR-12 was built up as a carbon fiber monocoque and clothed in carbon fiber composite panels for lightness and strength, weighing in at under 1,000 kilograms. The 60-degree V-12 engine was mounted amidships longitudinally and was of all-aluminum construction, normally aspirated via a Bosch

Zytek fuel-injection system. There were five speeds in the gearbox and double-wishbone suspension front and rear, with pushrod-actuated coil springs and shock absorbers. With more than 700 bhp on tap and a top speed of nearly 230 miles per hour, it needed the ventilated carbon disc brakes to stop it at the end of the straights.

In 1989 the car was returned to the UK to be prepared for Le Mans. In XJR-9LM spec, it was fitted with the 7.0-liter engine and revised engine covers, repainted in the new sponsor's (Silk Cut) colors. The car entered Le Mans but retired after just 85 laps. It then went back to the United States and into the Castrol livery for the US racing season, where it scored a solitary win at Tampa before returning again to Europe and its purple Silk Cut color scheme for the now historic victory at Le Mans in 1990.

XJR-12

Years of Production: 1990–1991
Engine: 6,995cc V-12 cylinder
Output: 730 horsepower
Top Speed: 229 miles per hour
Number Built: 5

Did You Know?

Chilean driver Eliseo Salazar, who was summarily dumped out of the winning XJR-12 at Le Mans by Tom Walkinshaw in 1990, started his career in Formula One, where he once ended up in a trackside fight with race leader Nelson Piquest after an overtaking maneuver. The fight ended up taking them both out of the 1982 German Grand Prix.

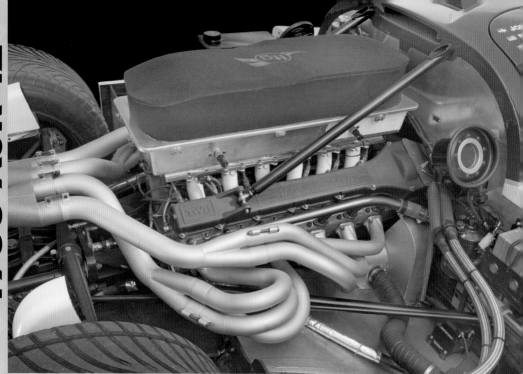

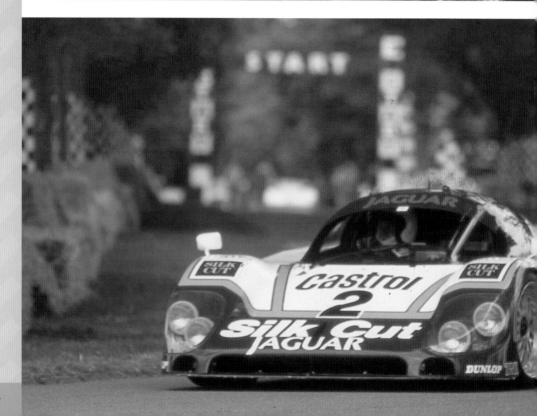

CHAPTER 8
THE FORD YEARS

In 1990 Jaguar was sold to United States manufacturer Ford, and swinging cuts were brought about to make the company profitable. About a third of the workforce lost their jobs. Ford, no stranger to racing, did not throw the baby out with the bathwater. It capitalized on Jaguar's recent motorsport successes, continuing the relationship with Tom Walkinshaw Racing and entering a pair of XJR-12s in the Daytona 24-hour race. At the finish, the winning Jaguar, driven by United States star Davy Jones, plus Jan Lammers and Andy Wallace, was four laps ahead of the Jaguar in second place. The racing team also went to Le Mans with the XJR-12, completing a memorable first and second at the world's most famous long-distance race and securing the company's seventh victory. They returned the following year to La Sarthe and, although missing out on the top spot to the incredible rotary-engined Mazda 787B, finished second, third, and fourth—a remarkable achievement.

All this success on the track was a good distraction for the company as they worked hard to develop new models to take over from the rather tired XJ Series. In the background, another project was moving forward in the workshop at Whitely Road on Coventry—the remarkable XJ220, started as an idea by members of The Saturday Club, who worked in their own time to come up with a supercar for the 1990s. The XJ220 concept model had already been launched on the Jaguar stand at the motor show at Earl's Court, and Ford now committed to putting it into production with TWR building it.

They would also make the extraordinary XJR-15 road car and race car, creating great press for the parent with minimum expense. There were facelifts for the XJS with the adoption of the AJ6 4.0-liter engine, and the range was further extended with the introduction of the 4.0-liter convertible. The last XJ6 Series III rolled off the production line in 1992, with sales of more than 400,000, while the XJ12, now named Jaguar Sovereign, was given another lease on life with a more powerful, refined, and economical 6.0-liter version of the V-12 engine.

In 1996 Jaguar released its first new sports car in a generation, the XK8 coupe and convertible. At the heart of the XK8 was an all-new AJ-V8 engine designed and developed at Whitley. The 4.0-liter, 290-bhp, 32-valve, quad cam V-8 was to be a good investment for Ford and used across its other brands, including Land Rover, Aston Martin, and Lincoln in the United States. The eagerly awaited S-Type was launched in 1998 to much acclaim. It was built in Jaguar's Castle Bromwich factory in Birmingham, which received more than £200 million worth of investment to bring it up to date for the new model. The new car was positioned in the range below the new XJ luxury model, which had been introduced in 1997 in a mold similar to the MK II, as a more affordable sporting saloon.

Jaguar unveiled a new interpretation of the classic roadster at the Paris Motor Show in 1998, 50 years after the company launched the XK engine and the XK120 sports car—the XK180 concept, styled by Keith Helfet. The XK180 was created to showcase the skills and talents of Jaguar designers, craftsmen, and engineers, and although not intended for production, it was based on a shortened version of the supercharged XKR convertible and fully functional—a forward glimpse of the F-Type still many years away. The AJ-V8 power unit was modified to produce 450 horsepower, with the brakes, wheels, and suspension upgraded to match the engine's performance.

Jaguar also announced its intention to enter Formula One. It purchased Jackie Stewart's team, Stewart F1, and signed Eddie Irvine and Johnny Herbert for the 2000 season. The team was to be called Jaguar Racing and the new car, the Jaguar R1, was launched to the press at a ceremony in London in January 2000. Despite huge investment by the parent company, the Jaguar F1 experience was not a happy one for Ford. In over 85 starts, its highest placing was only third with Irvine in Monaco in 2001, even though they had brought in three-time world champion Niki Lauda to advise the team. In 2004 it was sold to a drink manufacturer, Bull Racing.

A new executive saloon, code-named X300 during development, was launched at the Geneva Motor Show in 2001 and built at Ford's old Merseyside plant, Halewood. The X-Type featured a range of brand-new transverse V-6 engines of 2.5 or 3.0 liters and, all new for Jaguar, a four-wheel-drive model. In 2003 the new XJ X350 range was launched, replacing the X308 series.

The X350 was completely re-engineered, representing a breakthrough in aluminum monocoque design while preserving the traditional styling of the XJ line. The use of aluminum reduced the model's weight by 40 percent, increased its stiffness by 60 percent, and produced dramatic improvements in the vehicle's economy, ride, and handling. The new 3.0-liter AJ-V6 engine effectively replaced the 3.2-liter V-8, enabling a revival of the XJ6 badge.

However, a global economic crisis was looming, and the devaluation of the US dollar against the pound meant that Ford's Jaguar problems were exacerbated with losses rising into the millions. Saving money became the order of the day, and the consequences were severe.

After nearly 55 years of production at Browns Lane, the last cars rolled off its production lines in August 2005. It marked the end of the XK8, which soon would be replaced by the XK, to be built at Castle Bromwich along with the existing XJ. The new XK was introduced in 2006 as an updated model from the XK8, but was quite different. It followed the same aluminum monocoque path as the XJ350 with its new curvaceous lines penned by Jaguar's chief designer, Ian Callum.

Some of the most famous cars in the world had been produced at Browns Lane, including the XK120, C- and D-Types, Mk II, E-Type, XJ, and XJS. For many it was and would always be the spiritual home of Jaguar. And its closing was a sign of the times for Ford's ownership of the Jaguar brand.

The XK8 arose from Jaguar's urgent need to develop a new car on a limited budget. It used the existing XJS floorpan but with a new and more curvaceous body style, taking cues from both the classic E-Type and the XJ220 supercar. It was styled by Fergus Pollock and featured Jaguar's first-ever V-8 with variable valve timing for its incredibly complex 32-valve cylinder head, coupled to a five-speed ZF automatic transmission. The car used aircraft technology in its lightweight front subframe. Front and rear suspensions were also new, with an available

XK8

Years of Production: 1996–2006
Engine: DOHC 3,996cc 32-valve V-8
Output: 290–406 bhp
Top Speed: 155 miles per hour (limited)
Number Built: 91,406

electrically controlled adaptive damping system known as CATS. It came in two body styles, a coupe and a convertible, both designed as two-plus-two with leather and walnut throughout the cabin as you would expect in a Jaguar sports car.

Initially there was a problem with the Nikisil cylinder liners, and a product recall was made to correct the fault by reverting to steel liners.

In 1998 a supercharger was fitted on the XKR version, offering 370 bhp, and in 2004 the whole XK range underwent a styling facelift, with an enlarged frontal area, revised lighting, and side over-sills. Side rubbing strips were removed, and the rear bumper design was changed. New badging and exhaust systems were fitted according to model, with the XKR models getting a four-tailpipe system. A larger 4.2-liter engine was introduced in 2003, with 305 bhp for the normally aspirated car and a whopping 406 bhp on the supercharged XKR models. Both cars had standard speed limiters stopping the pull at 155 miles per hour. The XK8 and XKR first series went out of production in 2006 to make way for the new XK.

Did You Know?
The Jaguar XK8 shared a platform with the much more expensive Aston Martin DB7, hence the similar look.

The S-Type was introduced to the motoring press at the Birmingham Motor Show in 1998, reviving a name that had been absent from the Jaguar range since 1963—the old S-Type being a development of the Mark II. New styling by Geoff Lawson was very different from previous models, breaking with the Jaguar tradition of an almost seamless evolution from model to model within a range. It featured a wide selection of power units, from the new 2.5-liter V-6 with a diesel option and 3.0-liter gasoline V-6, effectively Ford's Duratec unit, to a 4.2-liter V-8 with the supercharged S-Type R completing the options in 2002.

There were five- and six-speed manual and automatic gearboxes with semi-automatic transmissions the only option on the V-8s. The blown edition, with a newly revised version of the Jaguar AJ-V8 engine, made 400 bhp with an Eaton supercharger and was capable of 0 to

60 in 5.3 seconds. With economies of scale in mind, Ford shared the S-Type platform across a number of their other brands, including the Lincoln LS and Ford DEW lines. There was a facelifted model in 2005 with an aluminum hood and modified grille. The last S-Type finally rolled off the production line at Jaguar's Castle Bromwich factory in 2007 to make way for the new XF.

S-TYPE

Years of Production: 1999–2008
Engines: 2,497cc V-6, 4,196cc V-8
Output: 197–400 bhp
Top Speed: 142–155 miles per hour (limited)
Number Built: 291,386

Did You Know?

Early S-Types featured the traditional leaping Jaguar hood ornament, specially engineered to break away in the case of an accident to comply with the US and EU standards. Later models had the badge in the radiator grille.

The XJ8 was one of the very last of the recognizable XJ range of cars that could trace its evolution right back to the very first XJ6 in 1968. The last Series III XJ6 was built in 1992, although the updated XJ40 had been available since 1986.

More than 300,000 XJ6s had been sold in its initial 24 years of production, and in true Jaguar tradition the lineage was apparent in the new XJ40, although squarer profiles at the corners and single headlights distinguished it from its predecessor. It was designed to have 25 percent fewer body panel pressings than the Series XJ, the new process saving weight, increasing stiffness of the chassis, and reducing cabin noise. Its successor in 1994 was the X300, and it harked back in styling to the earlier cars with the four round headlights at the front and a more curved nose. Otherwise, it was mechanically the same as the XJ30, featuring the solid AJ6 straight-six cylinder double-overhead camshaft engine. A supercharged

version called the XJR appeared in 1996, the first blown engine ever to feature in a Jaguar production car.

In 1997 the new AJ-V8 engine was fitted and the nomenclature changed to XJ8 to reflect the engine. It was available in two engine sizes, 3.2 and 4.0 liter, and there was another supercharged version of the 4.0-liter model. As a manual transmission had not been developed for the new engine, all were built with automatic gearboxes.

The Jaguar code-named X350 was introduced in 2004 with new all-aluminum body, saving a huge amount of weight and increasing performance. Built at Jaguar's Castle Bromwich plant, the new car now included the V-6 engine in the range and the XJ6 badge was returned to the back. The more powerful V-8 power units were still available, and a diesel 2.7-liter option was added later in the production run for Europe only. To improve the ride, air suspension was fitted all around, which provided adaptive damping as well as rear self-leveling, although it was automatic and could not be controlled by the driver.

XJ8

Years of Production: 2004–2009
Engines: 3.0-liter V-6, 4.2-liter V-8
Output: 240–300 bhp
Top Speed: 155 miles per hour
Number Built: 83,553

Did You Know?

There was one final incarnation of the recognizable XJ Series before its complete restyling in 2007, and it was also the most powerful. Called the Jaguar XJR, the supercharged Daimler version was christened the Super V8 and it produced a monstrous 400 bhp.

The new version of the XK8, the XK was unveiled in 2005 at the Frankfurt Motor Show. Its styling echoed Jaguar's most famous sports car, the E-Type, with its oval radiator aperture and indicated the start of Jaguar's resurgence by combining looks, handling, build quality, and performance. It featured the third generation of the all-aluminum quad cam 5.0-liter V-8 powerplant, incorporating spray-guided direct and dual independent variable cam timing and ZF six-speed automatic transmission. The new, normally aspirated engine is nearly as fast as the old XKR, with a 0–60 mile per hour sprint in 5.9 seconds, compared to the earlier car's 5.2, while top whack remains pegged at 155 miles per hour.

There were now electronic shock absorbers constantly adjusting the suspension, adapting to the road conditions. Jaguar's new suspension control unit, called Adaptive Dynamics, controlled vertical body movement as well as roll and pitch rates. It could be set to dynamic for a more sporty feel to the handling. Jaguar plainly hadn't forgotten that this was a GT car, not a pure sports car, and the firmer springs didn't disrupt the XK's excellent ride quality, enhanced by the 20-inch alloys. The double-wishbone front suspension was also comprehensively revised for greater levels of connection, feedback, and comfort.

Both the XK coupe and convertible body were manufactured out of lightweight metals

using engineering techniques developed in the aerospace industry, giving the XK's aluminum body exceptional stiffness while allowing pin-sharp cornering. Its green credentials weren't bad either, with over 25 miles per gallon and 50 percent of the body structure made from recycled aluminum. Modern touches included LED running lights, Xenon headlights, keyless entry, and the new pop-up JaguarDrive selector in the center console, along with a seven-inch touchscreen for the guidance system.

On the convertible, the roof mechanism was also redesigned, with opening and stowing in just 18 seconds. The XK collected the "best performance car" honor in a customer satisfaction survey of 36,000 owners in 2014, and was praised for its build and ride quality—not bad for a model at the end of its time. XK production ceased in July 2014 without a replacement model, as the F-Type took over the mantle as flagship sporting model.

XK

Years of Production: 2007–2014
Engine: 5.0-liter V-8
Output: 385 bhp
Top Speed: 158 miles per hour
Number Built: 56,837

Did You Know?

Jaguar's chief designer, Ian Callum, claimed that the inspiration for the shape of the new XK came from his admiration for British actress Kate Winslet's curves.

The XKR was the supercharged version of the Jaguar XK unveiled in 2007. It featured an Eaton supercharger bolted on to the already powerful all-alloy quad cam 5.0-liter V-8, boosting power from 385 bhp to over 500 bhp and adding more than 20 miles per hour to the top speed, bringing it to 174 miles per hour.

These supercharged XK variants also benefitted from Jaguar's Active Differential Control technology, which used a multi-plate clutch to manage the torque to the driven wheel with the most grip, allied to the ABS and stability control. The Active Differential was programmed to reduce steering sensitivity at the very high speeds of which the car was capable, increasing stability and driver control. Jaguar's software for Adaptive Damping was written for the XKR-S, ensuring extra stability and body control with maximum traction and grip.

The XKR was also upgraded with firmer springs and shock absorbers, lowered suspension, and a tweaked exhaust to be louder and crisper. Meatier steering and bigger brakes in its large 21-inch alloy wheels finished off the package.

Among a number of special editions was the XKR Goodwood Special in 2009, released at the Festival of Speed that year with its distinctive lime-green livery. In 2010 Jaguar launched a limited production of 75 XKR-75s

to celebrate the company's 75th anniversary. They delivered a combination of enhanced performance, stiffer chassis, and sharpened steering controls with increased grip levels to further probe the XKR's full potential.

The XKR-75 remained stable at high speeds thanks to a revised aerodynamic body pack and front splitter, side sill extensions, a rear diffuser, and larger rear spoiler, providing increased balance and reduced lift. Precise engine and transmission recalibration improved performance, while the regular XKR torque limiter, used to conserve gearbox life, was removed. Lowered ride height was conducive to track day driving on the European circuits, such as the fearsome Nurburgring. The cars were designed to complete fast laps, and then drive home again—reminiscent of the earliest days of Jaguar competition, pre-transports, when racers routinely drove their own competition vehicle to the track.

XKR

Years of Production: 2007–2014
Engine: 5.0-liter supercharged V-8
Output: 510 bhp
Top Speed: 174 miles per hour
Number Built: 21,487

Did You Know?

The XKR-S model was introduced in 2012 with an additional 40 horsepower over the XKR, bringing the 0–60 miles-per-hour time down to only 4.4 seconds. Top speed climbed to 186 miles per hour, making it the fastest production Jaguar yet, after the XJ220.

CHAPTER 9
MODERN CONCEPTS

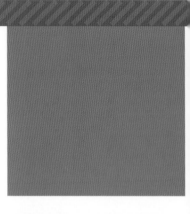

The R&D department is one of the most exciting spots in the automobile industry. Here physical laws, market forces, technical aspirations, and the dreams and passions of the designers themselves must clash and congeal, influenced or unimpinged by company priorities. Sometimes technology drives the process, such as the hybrid sector—or more radical notions, such as the C-X75's diesel turbine/electric power combination. Many concepts never make it past the drawing board stage, and fewer still survive to a solid mock-up. These early-stage designs, often closer to the designer's passions than the market's imputed demands, can become some of the most memorable cars that we revere today. The XJ220 captivated the public as an exhibition car, bearing lines The Saturday Club had penned while daydreaming of a thrilling modern sports car.

The XJ220 retained many of the lines that it was first penned with, and it can be argued that this simple, first vision approach is the best way to design a car rather than the unlimited options that CAD offers today. William Lyons—master of the clean-sheet approach—certainly thought so, and he styled many of the most iconic models that Jaguar's foundations were built upon. He strongly believed in evolution of design, and you can see the lineage clearly in most Jaguars as they develop one model from the next. Sometimes these are small changes, and at others giant leaps of faith either in styling, as with the XK120, or in engineering, as with the XJ12's glorious all-alloy V-12 engine.

Starting with the stylist's drawings, a small-scale model is made, and if approved a full-scale styling buck follows. This can be made in a number of materials—traditionally wood, but now more likely resin or clay—which can be further shaped to perfect the lines. If it's to be seen by the public, at a motor show or sibling product launch, it gets paint, glass, and trim, such as door handles, grille, badges, and wheels. Still a solid base, like the C-X75 styling buck photographed here, there are no mechanicals. If the press receives the new concept well, the company may build up a full prototype, but many never get past this stage. The back lots of automobile companies around the world are packed with stored concepts that never made it to the road. Mostly, these lavishly styled concepts give us a clue about what is to come in the years ahead. They are like the haute couture on the catwalk of the fashion world, not practical but designed to inspire us and accentuate the brand.

2010 C-X75

Jaguar unveiled the C-X75 in 2010. It was the beginning of a new chapter in innovation and technological advancement that would see the car evolve from a design concept to a fully working prototype in just two years.

Introduced to the press at the Paris Motor Show, its name reflects Jaguar's 75th anniversary. It was styled by chief designer Ian Callum, who looked toward the XJ13 and XJ220 for inspiration. In that incredibly short time span, Jaguar and development partner Williams Advanced Engineering created an all-wheel-drive, plug-in parallel hybrid electric vehicle (PHEV) with the world's highest specific power engine and Jaguar's first carbon composite monocoque chassis.

C-X75

Year of Production: 2010
Engine: four electric motors charged by two diesel turbines
Output: 778 bhp
Top Speed: 205 miles per hour
Number Built: 5

The C-X75 had a combined power output in excess of 850 bhp, thanks to its state-of-the-art, Formula One-inspired, 1.6-liter dual-boosted (turbocharged and supercharged) four-cylinder powerplant, which generates 502 bhp at 10,000 rpm. There are also four electric motors, one for each wheel, and the batteries are charged by the two diesel turbines. The electric motors

generate a further 390 bhp, and the battery pack in the C-X75 is the highest continuously rated power PHEV pack in the world, capable of delivering more than 300 kilowatts.

The C-X75 can accelerate from 0–100 miles per hour in less than six seconds, thanks to its advanced seven-speed automated manual transmission that allows gearshifts in under 200 milliseconds. The very first C-X75 prototype exceeded 200 miles per hour in testing with ease, and the car has a theoretical maximum velocity of 220 miles per hour.

Deployable aerofoil and under-floor aerodynamics create more than 200 kilograms of downforce at 200 miles per hour, and Jaguar's own active systems enhance its high-speed stability. Thanks to the most extreme PHEV specification of any mobile battery in development, the C-X75 can also run for 60 kilometers in pure electric vehicle mode.

The original plan was to build a limited-run production of C-X75, featuring a gasoline engine and costing more than $1 million, in conjunction with the Williams F1 team. Sadly, Jaguar decided in 2012 that as a result of the global economic climate, the C-X75 would not enter full production.

The C-X75 powertrain technologies and lightweight composites demonstrated Jaguar's technical leadership at the very cutting edge of automotive development and manufacturing. The C-X75 concept represents the pinnacle of Jaguar's engineering and design expertise and is arguably the world's fastest testbed for the world's most advanced technologies, combining hybrid powertrain with awe-inspiring performance. Jaguar has always looked to shape the cars of tomorrow, and with projects like C-X75, they are laying down the foundations for the next generation of Jaguar cars to build upon.

> ### Did You Know?
> The C-X75 will feature in the new 2015 James Bond film, *Spectre*.

Jaguar's C-X16 was a two-seater hybrid sports car concept unveiled at the Frankfurt Motor Show in 2011. It showed Jaguar's vision for a true twenty-first century sports car and was a sign of the F-Type to come. The beautiful lines penned by Ian Callum include superb details, such as flush door handles with built-in touch sensors that trigger silent electric motors to present the machined aluminum handles to driver and passenger.

The C-X16 was driven by a prototype hybrid powertrain, featuring a supercharged, all-alloy V-6 engine with independently rotating balancer weights at the front and rear of the engine for smooth running, and an electric motor producing an additional 70 kilowatts. Driving the rear wheels through an eight-speed transmission, this hybrid powertrain gives the lightweight C-X16 the potential to accelerate to 62 miles per hour in 4.4 seconds and reach a top speed of 186 miles per hour. With perfect 50:50 weight distribution, this system pointed the way to the next generation of enhanced, efficient, powerful internal combustion engines that Jaguar would develop.

This hybrid technology reduced fuel consumption and allowed the car to run as a zero-tailpipe-emissions electric vehicle at speeds of up to 50 miles per hour. A burst of extra electric power was instantaneously available by pushing a button on the steering wheel.

The new V-6 engine used the same lightweight aluminum architecture as the eight-cylinder with a high-pressure, diecast block with cross-bolted main bearing caps for increased strength and refinement. The dual cam, four-valve cylinder heads were constructed with recycled aluminum to reduce the environmental impact of manufacturing.

The C-X16 concept was fitted with Jaguar's Intelligent Stop/Start, which shuts down the engine 300 milliseconds after the car has stopped. First launched in the XF, the system uses a Twin Solenoid Starter that is capable of restarting it in the time it takes the driver's foot to travel from the brake to the accelerator.

C-X16 (F-TYPE HYBRID)

Year of Production: 2011
Engine: supercharged 3.0-liter V-6 DOHC four-valve gasoline/electric motor
Output: 380 bhp + 70kW
Top Speed: 186 miles per hour
Number Built: 1

Did You Know?

The C-X16 featured an on-demand short burst of power and acceleration. Known as "Push to Pass," this let the driver increase the car's power by 70 kilowatts for a burst of up to 10 seconds, inspired by Formula One KERS systems.

Project 7, created by a team led by Director of Design Ian Callum, is a one-off design study based on the acclaimed new Jaguar F-Type. It acknowledges Jaguar's winning Le Mans seven times from 1951 to 1990, a record for a British manufacturer.

Following digital modeling, a clay model of Project 7 was produced from an experimental sketch by Jaguar designer Cesar Pieri. The fully functional sports car was completed and ready for testing in just four months, its blue paintwork reminiscent of the victorious Jaguar D-Types of 1956–1957. Key exterior

PROJECT 7

Year of Production: 2013
Engine: supercharged 5.0-liter V-8
Output: 550 bhp
Top Speed: 186 miles per hour
Number Built: 1

design changes included a fairing behind the driver's head, custom carbon fiber components, new front splitter, side skirts and rear diffuser, lowered windshield, and restyled front bumper.

Designed as a single-seater roadster, the Project 7 featured a Jaguar D-Type-inspired

fairing, carbon fiber aerodynamic touches, and a unique interior featuring a composite single seat with racing harness and helmet holder.

The F-Type's rigid all-aluminum architecture provided the perfect base, with power coming from Jaguar's 5.0-liter supercharged V-8 engine with more than 500 bhp. Project 7 can reach 60 miles per hour in 4.1 seconds, with a top speed of 186 miles per hour, and has a Carbon Ceramic Braking System to stop it. Power is delivered to the rear wheels through Jaguar's eight-speed Quickshift automatic transmission and an electronic active differential.

In a surprise announcement, Jaguar confirmed that it will build a limited run of 250 F-Type Project 7 road cars. These will be two-seater versions of the prototype car, but will have even more power at 575 bhp, accelerating to 0–60 in just 3.8 seconds. They will be built by Special Operations and will be the most powerful production Jaguar ever made.

Did You Know?

A very similar looking prototype appeared in 1999, called the XK180. It was based on the XK8, but had a much higher top speed of 180 miles per hour.

The C-X17 is a brand-new sports crossover concept that Jaguar has been working on for a number of years to take full advantage of the close relationship with Land Rover's expertise with all-wheel-drive technology.

Designed from the ground up, the C-X17 is being developed with an eye to the rapidly expanding Chinese market. The Jaguar spiel says, "As a luxurious sports crossover, the latest C-X17 concept stretches the design possibilities of the segment by combining the character and driving experience of a luxury sports car with increased presence, style and flexibility."

There will be a range of engines, including brand-new high-output, fuel-efficient gasoline

C-X17 (F-PACE 4X4)
Year of Production: 2015
Engine: four-cylinder, V-6 gasoline
Output: 280 bhp estimate
Top Speed: estimate 175 miles per hour
Number Built: 1

and diesel units to be built at Jaguar Land Rover's upcoming UK engine manufacturing facility, in which they are investing more than £500 million.

The C-X17 concept study showcases the next generation of lightweight technologies in the form of Jaguar's all-new advanced aluminum monocoque, which will

form the basis for a new range of future Jaguars. The interior is luxuriously appointed, featuring Connolly leather panels. Two additional rear-mounted leisure seats, incorporated into the wood-lined trunk floor, swing out for recreational use. Accessories that support an active lifestyle, such as a portable light and a camera, are positioned in storage compartments in the trunk.

The C-X17 concept has an on-road bias, and its low height, optimized center of gravity, and lightweight body offer a more car-like driving experience, both in urban environments and out on the open road. It also features cutting-edge technologies, such as torque

vectoring—a system that monitors the vehicle's cornering dynamics and, when required, intelligently uses the brake system to rebalance the distribution of engine torque to individual wheels, in order to reduce understeer, maximize grip, and enhance stability. The large 23-inch wheels, which show off the C-X17's solid stance, are a one-off, five-split-spoke design. The sculpted haunch lines echo those of the F-Type. The radiator grille features a hexagonal pattern, with small aluminum panels within its structure that can close to enhance the vehicle's aerodynamic properties, while the LED headlights, J-shaped running lights, and frosted-glass foglights emphasize its curvaceous shape. The C-X17 also has a unique full-size panoramic glass roof.

The new model features a brand-new rear-exit detection system that utilizes sensors to warn exiting passengers of quickly approaching hazards, such as cyclists and mopeds. When a passenger's hand touches the interior door handle, the system is activated, illuminating a hidden-until-lit icon in the pillar trim that identifies whether a hidden hazard is approaching.

A center tunnel running partway down the length of the cabin incorporates the innovative Interactive Surface Console, an infotainment hub with a series of touchscreens that work in conjunction with the secure in-car Wi-Fi network.

The instrument panel has a provision for a heads-up display to project vital information onto the windshield.

2015 C-X17 (F-PACE 4X4)

Did You Know?
The C-X17 is going be built as the F-Pace, which Jaguar calls a family sports car, blending style, performance, and practicality.

CHAPTER 10
TODAY'S RANGE OF JAGUARS

It's hard to relate the modern range of today's Jaguar cars to those first sporting saloons before World War II more than 70 years ago. But there is still a direct lineage that can be traced back through the Ford years' XK8 to the great XJ6 and XJ12 of the 1970s to the fabulous E-Type and the XK120 that spawned that double overhead cam straight-six engine. Through all of Jaguar's up and downs, with a stalled manufacturer beginning again after the war, to when it nearly lost its identity during the British Motor Corporation years and through the industrial disputes and lumbering inefficiencies that almost did in the company, one thing has remained strong: the Jaguar brand.

That brand was nurtured through the tough times by one man, William Lyons. It was his determination that rebuilt the company when hostilities ceased in 1945; it was his spirit that encouraged the competition department to ascend to the dizzy heights of seven Le Mans wins and countless other race and rally wins; and it was his vision that recognized what the public aspired to in a car and sold it to them.

Under Ford's ownership, Jaguar expanded its range of products with the launch of the S-Type in 1999 and X-Type in 2001 and invested heavily, which had been lacking in the decade before. Since Land Rover's May 2000 purchase by Ford, it has been closely associated with Jaguar. In many countries they share a common sales and distribution network (including shared dealerships), and some models now share components. This global view of automobile

manufacture is part of today's world, and the current owners at Tata Motors know all about it with their background firmly rooted in the developing world. Their approach to Jaguar has refreshed the brand beyond all expectations and taken many other car manufacturers by surprise, but they couldn't have done that without all the heritage to draw upon. That evolution of vision, design, and engineering is what makes Jaguar

stand out from the crowd. There is a link from one model to the next, often a small one and sometimes a giant leap, but it is there and you can't create that overnight. It flows from the venerable marque's history.

With Jaguar's XF and new XE models, the company has brought its sporting philosophy to cars in a sector that most of us would consider executive runabouts, but the Jaguar badge on

the grille makes for many aspiring owners. In the XJ, we see heads of state, managing directors, and rock stars being delivered to high-profile events, just as we did with those fabulous Daimler limousines of the 1960s and Jaguar XJ12 of the 1970s era.

The fantastic F-Type is admired throughout the world as a flagship sports car defining the brand just as the E-Type and XK120 had done in the past, and at a highly competitive price. The new aluminum monocoque architecture that the whole range of current models is based upon would not have been financially viable even a dozen years ago without the long-term investment and future thinking of engineers long gone from the company. Jaguar is definitely fighting fit and will be safe in the hands of Tata for a long while yet.

The first of the modern range of Jaguars was introduced to the press in 2007 at the Frankfurt Motor Show. Designed by Jaguar's chief designer, Ian Callum, using Computational Fluid Dynamics while still with the Ford family, the XF showed what the future of Jaguar cars would look like. It was only first seen as concept C-XF in January of that year and is built in Jaguar's Castle Bromwich factory, and more recently after Tata acquired the marque, in India in CKD (Completely Knocked Down) form.

There is a wide range of models varying in engine and trim level across pretty much any specification, from the four-cylinder diesel version introduced in 2012 and capable of 57 miles per gallon via a 3.0-liter V-6, to the

XF

Years of Production: 2007–present
Engines: 2.2-liter diesel, 5.0-liter gasoline supercharged
Output: 163–503 bhp
Top Speed: 186 miles per hour
Number Built: 173,376 so far

supercharged all-aluminum quad cam V-8 engine producing over 500 bhp. Unusually, the diesel engines have been produced in a joint venture with French company Peugeot-Citroen.

The aluminum chassis is a development from the S-Type and was launched with only an automatic eight-speed ZF gearbox aimed very much at the global company car market.

An all-wheel-drive option was introduced in some left-hand-drive markets only available with the supercharged 3.0-liter V-6 engine.

The sport brake station wagon was launched in 2012 with the whole range of engines on offer and more capacity in the trunk than the equivalent Mercedes or BMW models. The XF R-Sport saloon and sport brake were the first Jaguars to wear the new R-Sport badge. An active electronic differential and Jaguar's own dynamic stability control systems from the XFR-S Saloon beef up the XFR-S sport brake's handling characteristics, making it corner like the saloon.

In 2011, for the fourth successive year, the Jaguar XF won the What Car? Best Executive Car award. Interior features include air conditioning vents flush-fitting in the dash, rotating open once the engine is started, and a rotating gearshift dial called the Jaguar Drive Selector, which rises out of the center console. Another departure from the traditional Jaguar cabin is the pale-blue backlighting to the instruments and switchgear and around major control panels. Some minor systems, such as the interior lighting, are controlled simply by touching the light covers. Unusually, the XF has no cloth interior option, with even the entry-level model being fully trimmed in leather and wood veneer or optionally aluminum, carbon fiber, and piano black lacquer trim.

On November 7, 2008, a modified XFR was driven by Paul Gentilozzi of Rocketsports, who prepared the car, to a new Jaguar record of 225.675 miles per hour on the Bonneville Salt Flats. The new record beat the previous Jaguar record of 217.1 miles per hour in an XJ220 in 1992.

Did You Know?

Jaguar makes a special emergency services version of the XF diesel, used by the police in the UK. It features a roof-mounted light bar, blue and white strobing LEDs in the grille, and blue flashing LEDs along the side of the car and the rear light clusters.

First revealed at the 2012 Paris Motor Show, the F-Type is the natural successor to the E-Type, and like that icon it defines the current Jaguar brand. It is based on a shortened XK chassis and features an all-aluminum lightweight monocoque with the rear wheels driving the car via a wide range of power units. The convertible was the first production car to appear in 2013, with the coupe following the next year. But the idea may be traced back years earlier to January 2000, when Jaguar's F-Type concept roadster was unveiled at the North American International Auto Show in Detroit. Design work had commenced under the direction of Geoff Lawson, Jaguar's director of styling, who sadly died in June 1999. The project was completed by the new director of design, Ian Callum.

There are three models available, the F-Type, F-Type S, and F-Type V-8 S. The range-topping F-Type V-8 S will reach 60 miles per hour in 4.2 seconds and has a top speed of 186 miles per hour.

The asymmetric interior is still luxurious by other sports car standards, with touchscreen displays in the center console, leather and wooden paneling, and metal finishes. There is special anti-vibration insulation provided

by rubber engine mounts, which reduce road noise along with a double bulkhead between the engine bay and passenger compartment. Both front and rear suspension systems are all-aluminum double-wishbone configuration, providing precise road holding.

The ZF gearbox uses eight closely spaced sporting ratios featuring Jaguar's own Quickshift transmission with paddle shifters offering manual override. Fully adjustable suspension settings allow the driver to choose ride and handling qualities from among 25 different modes programmed to suit different road conditions and driving styles. Torsional and lateral stiffness in the aluminum monocoque have been improved for handling agility, and there is a quick-ratio steering rack for rapid turn-in. The F-Type core body-in-white weighs just 561 pounds (261 kilograms) with the whole car tipping the scales at just 3,520 pounds (1,597 kilograms). Use of more composite materials in the F-Type than in any previous Jaguar car help keep it light on the scales.

Distinctive styling cues include shark-like gills on either side of the grille, power bulge on the clamshell hood, and deployable door handles and rear spoiler—the latter reducing lift at speed by up to 264 pounds (120 kilograms). The S and V-8 S versions also feature an "active exhaust system" that opens special valves over 3,000 rpm to intensify the sound.

In 2015, the F-Type introduced the ZF six-speed manual, the transmission being only available for the V-6 models alongside a mechanical limited slip differential on the V-6 S and an electronic limited slip differential on the V-8.

F-TYPE

Years of Production: 2013–present
Engines: 3.0-liter V-6, 5.0-liter V-8 (both supercharged)
Output: 335–550 bhp
Top Speed: 186 miles per hour
Number Built: not released by Jaguar

Did You Know?

As part of the F-Type launch, a short film entitled *Desire*, directed by Adam Smith from Ridley Scott Associates and featuring the car, was shown in April 2013 at the Sundance Film Festival. It starred Damian Lewis from the hit TV series *Homeland*.

The new Jaguar sports saloon, the XE (code-name X760), is available in 2015, initially as a saloon although estate and coupe models are thought to be in the pipeline. An all-wheel-drive version of the XE is expected be launched in 2016.

The XE is the first compact executive Jaguar since the 2009 X-Type. It is also the first of several Jaguar models to be built using Jaguar's new modular aluminum architecture—marking the departure from the Ford-derived platforms used for the X-Type and XF. Jaguar's platform features rear-wheel-drive and

XE

Years of Production: 2015–present
Engines: turbo 2.0-liter gasoline and diesel S4, 3.0-liter supercharged V-6, 5.0-liter supercharged V-8
Output: 161–490 bhp
Top Speed: 140–155 miles per hour
Number Built: figures not released by Jaguar

all-wheel-drive configurations, and it is the first car in its segment with an aluminum monocoque structure built at the new Jaguar Land Rover factory in Solihull. The new Ingenium 2.0-liter four-cylinder engines

are built at another new engine plant near Wolverhampton and will be shared with Land Rover models. The body was designed by Ian Callum and his team. It is the most aerodynamic Jaguar ever made, with a drag coefficient of just 0.26.

In the cabin, front- and rear-seat occupants have a generous amount of headroom and legroom. The Jaguar rotary gear selector controls the eight-speed ZF automatic transmission, plus, as seen in the XF, there is a six-speed manual gearbox available on diesel models.

The dash features an eight-inch touchscreen to control in-car entertainment, satellite navigation, and vehicle settings. The XE is also able to connect with smartphones, and some models allow the owner to control the vehicle remotely, preheating the interior or unlocking the car using a smartphone application. A color heads-up display is also fitted to project speed and navigation instructions onto the windshield in front of the driver.

All suspension components are manufactured from aluminum using Jaguar's double-wishbone suspension at the front, complemented by an entirely new subframe and multi-link suspension at the rear. A new traction-control system developed with expertise from Jaguar's sister brand, Land Rover, allows for better handling in snow and ice.

The safest Jaguar ever built, the XE also features an advanced emergency-braking system that will detect situations where the relative speed and distance between vehicles suggest that a collision is imminent. In such a situation, emergency braking can be automatically applied to avoid the collision or mitigate its effects.

Did You Know?

Jaguar's Special Operations division will prepare a high-performance variant with the supercharged V-8 to compete with the Audi RS4 and BMW M3.